WHO IS THE ANTICHRIST?

MARK HITCHCOCK

HARVEST HOUSE PUBLISHERS

EUGENE, OREGON

Cover by Left Coast Design, Portland, Oregon

Cover photos © Nathaniel Gilera Hayag Photography / Flickr / Getty Images; Maciej Toporowicz, NYC / Flickr / Getty Images

Published in association with William K. Jensen Literary Agency, 119 Bampton Court, Eugene, Oregon 97404

WHO IS THE ANTICHRIST?
Copyright © 2011 by Mark Hitchcock
Published by Harvest House Publishers
Eugene, Oregon 97402
www.harvesthousepublishers.com

Library of Congress Cataloging-in-Publication Data
Hitchcock, Mark.
Who is the Antichrist? / Mark Hitchcock.
    p. cm.
ISBN 978-0-7369-3995-9 (pbk.)
ISBN 978-0-7369-4204-1 (eBook)
1. Antichrist. I. Title.
BT985.H59 2011
236—dc22
                                                                2010046907

To Jay Risner,
a faithful friend and colaborer for Christ.

Thanks for your godly example and influence
on my sons and for your heart for
our Lord and His church.

Who Is the Antichrist?

Answering the Question Everyone Is Asking

"When Satan tempted Jesus in the wilderness, he offered Jesus all the kingdoms of the world if He would bow down and worship him. Of course, Jesus refused his offer. But in the future there is coming a man who will take Satan up on the offer, and whom Satan will indwell, giving his power, throne, and all his authority into the hands of this one man."

DONALD GREY BARNHOUSE

PART I

The Curiosity About the Antichrist

———○———

"Many people believe the great millennial end-game has already begun. As civilization speeds toward its final destiny, the appearance of a powerful world ruler is inevitable. The ultimate question facing our generation is whether he is already alive and well and moving into power."

ED HINDSON, *IS THE ANTICHRIST ALIVE AND WELL?*

Why is there so much interest in and speculation about the Antichrist today?

I heard a story a while back about two Jehovah's Witnesses who were going door-to-door and hoping for the opportunity to talk to people about their views. They came to the door of a man who invited them in and asked them to take a seat in the living room while he took care of something in the back room. After a few minutes the man returned to the living room and said, "Now what was it you wanted to talk to me about?" Surprised, the two Jehovah's Witnesses looked at each other. Then one of them said, "We don't know. We've never been this far before."

That's an accurate illustration of where people find themselves today with regard to the future: We've never been this far before. In Romans 13:11-12 we read, "Do this, knowing the time, that it is already the hour for you to awaken from sleep; for now salvation is nearer to us than when we believed. The night is almost gone, and the day is near."

It is becoming increasingly clear to many that this world is drawing nearer to "closing time," and people are asking questions about the future like never before. Many are fearful, anxious, and uncertain. There's a growing fascination with what might happen next. People are more and more focused on what tomorrow might hold. Economic meltdowns, the menace of pandemic plagues, cataclysmic natural disasters, and the dreaded threat of nuclear terror are all converging to make the world a more dangerous place than at any other time in human history.

At the same time, there's growing talk among world leaders about efforts toward global unity. For example, there have been high-profile economic and climate conferences at which government representatives have tried to get multiple countries to work together toward certain goals. And there are other ways that various governments have called for global cooperation with regard to specific problems and issues. More and more we are seeing efforts toward a centralization of power that is leading many to wonder if the time of the Antichrist is here—if the final world ruler and his one-world government is about to make his debut on the world stage. The world is longing for someone who can bring hope and provide answers for the world's mounting crises. Could the Antichrist's arrival be soon—very soon? Could he be alive now and present somewhere on earth, waiting in the wings for his time to come?

People are talking about the Antichrist more and more these

days. In some ways this is not surprising because people have always had a fascination with the human personification of evil, and they've had a heyday trying to figure out who the Antichrist is. The identity of the Antichrist has intrigued people for 2000 years, and many have found the temptation to identify him irresistible. Through the centuries, they've suggested numerous possibilities, and one consistent candidate has been the various popes. Martin Luther, the great reformer, is reported to have said, "I feel much freer now that I am certain the pope is the Antichrist."

Among the more prominent candidates that have been suggested are Emperor Frederick II, Pope Innocent IV, Muhammad, the Turks, Napoleon, Hitler, Mussolini, and Stalin. In more recent times there's been no shortage of names:

President John F. Kennedy—He was a Catholic who was assassinated by a head wound. Some people associated this with the mortal wound the Antichrist will one day receive (see Revelation 13:3) and expected Kennedy to come back to life.

Henry Kissinger—He is a Jewish person whose name, according to some calculations, equals 666. A key reason some people suggested he might be the Antichrist was his former renown as a great diplomat and peacemaker.

Mikhail Gorbachev—Who could ignore that great red mark on his forehead? Some people assumed it just had to be related to the mark of the beast.

President Ronald Reagan—His name, Ronald Wilson Reagan, was comprised of three words with six letters each, which some people equated with the number 666. They also thought his recovery from a gunshot wound might have some significance.

Bill Clinton—Many people pointed to Bill Clinton as possibly being the Antichrist, and some of them viewed Hillary as the false prophet (a companion of the Antichrist who, according to

the book of Revelation, will promote Antichrist's power and per-
suade people to worship him).

Some people have jokingly referred to this ongoing effort
to identify the Antichrist as "pin the tail on the Antichrist." It's
worth observing that those who engage in this exercise generally
pin the Antichrist moniker on whomever they happen to partic-
ularly dislike. Almost every president since Ronald Reagan has
been identified as the Antichrist by someone. So it's not too surprising that after Barack Obama became president, some began
to suggest he is the Antichrist. There are cable news programs that
have run interviews and stories about this claim, and polls show
that this isn't merely some lunatic fringe belief. According to a
Louis Harris poll taken on March 23, 2010,

- 67 percent of Republicans (and 40 percent of Americans
  overall) believe that Obama is a socialist

- 45 percent of Republicans (and 25 percent overall) believe that Obama was "not born in the United States and
  so is not eligible to be president"

- 38 percent of Republicans (and 20 percent overall) say
  that Obama is "doing many of the things that Hitler did"

But the most intriguing finding of all is that 24 percent of Republicans (and 14 percent of Americans overall) say that Obama
"may be the Antichrist." Those who hold this view have been
dubbed "Antichristers," just as those who have questioned President Obama's citizenship are called "birthers."[1]

The specter of Obama as the Antichrist has circulated widely
on the Internet. There's a video that's acquired quite a following that maintains Jesus gave us the name of the Antichrist and
links Barack Obama to the name, although a disclaimer is given
that the narrator is not claiming that President Obama is the

Antichrist. The video is based on Luke 10:18, where Jesus said, "I was watching Satan fall from heaven like lightning." The argument then progresses like this:

1. Jesus spoke in Aramaic, not Greek.

2. Jesus said, "I saw Satan falling as lightning from the heights, or from the heavens."

3. The passage is then retranslated as "I saw Satan falling as lightning from the heavens."

4. It's noted that in biblical Hebrew, the word translated "lightning" is *baraq*.

5. This is related to Isaiah 14, which speaks of Satan or Lucifer.

6. The Hebrew translated "heights" in Isaiah 14:14 is *bamaw*.[2]

Well, you can see where this is headed. Is there any validity to that line of thinking? The best analysis of this reasoning has been done by New Testament scholar Daniel B. Wallace. After addressing each of the above points and several more, Wallace reached this conclusion:

> When all is said and done, the evidence is simply bogus. Jesus didn't speak in Hebrew, and the Hebrew that is given here does not mean "lightning from the heights." *Baraq ubamah* means "lightning and height." But that can hardly be the underlying Aramaic (which is not Hebrew) for the Greek text of Luke 10:18. Thus, a linguistic leap from Greek to Aramaic to Hebrew, with the grammar and vocabulary changing along the way, is required to make Luke 10:18 mean what the narrator wants it to mean.[3]

Much was said in some circles about the claim that the winning lottery number in the Pick 3 lottery in the President's home state (Illinois) on November 5, 2008, the day after his presidential election victory, was 6-6-6. Others have said that his zip code is 60606. One blogger noted, "Why are there so many coincidences with Obama and 666?" and then went on to list the alleged "coincidences."

> Birth date: August 4 (216th day of the year)
> 216 = 6 x 6 x 6
>
> Birthplace: Longtitude 21.6 (again the number 216)
> 216 (21.6) = 6 x 6 x 6
>
> Name: 18 letters
> 18 = 6 + 6 + 6
>
> The winning lottery ticket number in Chicago, Obama's home governing state the day after he was elected was…
> 6-6-6
>
> The next pick was…
> 7-7-7-9
>
> According to God's numerology…
> 666 = Antichrist
> 777= Perfect completion
> 9 = Judgment
> 6667779 = "Antichrist perfect completion judgment (time?)"[4]

I have no idea whether all those allegations are true, but it shows the extent to which some people are obsessed with trying to figure out the identity of the Antichrist. Not long after all the furor about Obama was hitting the mainstream, an extremist group called the Hutaree militia got a lot of attention in the news because they had plotted to murder a police officer and then kill the mourners at his funeral with the help of homemade bombs. All this was part of a grand plan to prepare for battle with the Antichrist. A key part of the theology concocted by this group was a belief that former NATO secretary-general Javier Solana is the Antichrist.[5]

Another reason for the high level of interest people have in the Antichrist stems from the presence of an Antichrist figure in many world religions. You might be surprised, as I was, to learn that the three great world religions (Christianity, Judaism, and Islam) teach about a powerful and sinister world ruler who will emerge during the end times. They are all looking for a man of unparalleled evil, an ultimate enemy who will come during the last days and take over the world.

In Islam, this person is called *Al-Dajjal,* which in Arabic means "deceiver." His full title is *Al-Maseeh* (the Messiah) *Ad-Dajjal,* (the Liar/Deceiver). Here are some of his main characteristics, according to Islamic teaching:

- He will be a young man.
- He will appear during a time of great tribulation.
- He will be blind in one eye (there are conflicting sources about which eye), and this eye will be covered by a thick film while the other eye will bulge out and protrude like a floating grape.
- He will have thick hair.
- He will have the word *Infidel* (*Kaafir*) written in between his eyes, or possibly on his forehead, but only true Muslims will perceive its meaning.
- The Dajjal will possess incredible supernatural powers that he will use to deceive Muslims. According to one source, "The Dajjal will have powers of the devil. He will terrorize the Muslims into following him, converting

them into unbelief. He will conceal the truth and bring forth falsehood. The prophet said that the Dajjal will have the power to show the image of one's dead ancestors on his hand, like a television screen. The relative will say, 'Oh my son! This man is correct. I am in Paradise because I was good and I believed in him.' In reality that relative is in hell. If the relative says, 'Believe in this man; I am in hell because I didn't believe,' one must say to the Dajjal, 'No, he is in Paradise. This is false.'"[6]

- He will be the incarnation of evil.

- He will claim to be God.

- He will be a Jew who will gather 70,000 Jewish followers, along with other nonbelievers and hypocrites.

- He will go on a whirlwind tour of deception and destruction.

- He will set himself up as ruler in Jerusalem.

- He will finally be slain by Jesus at the Lydda Gate when the latter returns from heaven.

- The Dajjal's emergence on the world scene is one of Islam's ten key signs of the end times.

Judaism also has an Antichrist figure. Judaism teaches that a Roman ruler named Armilus will be a miracle worker who will lead his armies against Jerusalem. In the end, Armilus will be killed by Messiah ben David or Messiah the Son of David, the true Messiah.

In Christianity, as we have already seen, this final world ruler is known as the Antichrist, the beast, and the man of sin, as well as several other names and titles.

When we consider that three of the world's great religions are looking for the rise of a great political-religious leader in the end times, it's no surprise today that speculation about the Antichrist's identity is on the rise. In fact, there is rapidly growing speculation that he may already be here. And people want to know who he is. I believe that as the world's problems continue to worsen, the curiosity will become all the more intense. With all that's transpiring in our world today, people are asking questions about the end times and the Antichrist like never before. Questions like:

- Are events in our world today setting the stage for the Antichrist's appearance?
- Who is this satanic superman who is yet to burst on the world scene?
- Where will he come from?
- What will he be like, and what will he do?
- Will he appear during our lifetime?

These are the kinds of questions I hope to answer throughout this book as we endeavor to answer the big question that stands as the title for this book: Who is the Antichrist?

Why should I be concerned about the Antichrist?

When it comes to thinking about the Antichrist, some people today may feel like Denis the Carthusian, who said, "Have we not worn ourselves out with that accursed Antichrist?"[7] Yet I believe there are at least four reasons we should take the time to inform ourselves about the coming Antichrist.

First, the Bible has a great deal to tell us about this final world ruler. Other than Jesus Christ, the main person in all of Bible prophecy and all of human history is the coming world ruler or

Antichrist. My friend Dr. Harold Willmington aptly described the uniqueness of the future world dictator. As you can tell from the numbers in the following quote he made this statement some years ago, but the idea still holds true: "Since the days of Adam, it has been estimated that approximately 40 billion human beings have been born upon our earth. Four and one-half billion of this number are alive today. However, by any standard of measurement one might employ, the greatest human (apart from the Son of God himself) in matters of ability and achievement is yet to make his appearance upon our planet."[8]

Few people probably realize that there are more than 100 passages of Scripture that describe the origin, nationality, character, career, kingdom, and final doom of the Antichrist. He is discussed at length in the Old Testament book of Daniel as well as in the New Testament books of 2 Thessalonians and Revelation. God doesn't want us to be preoccupied with this individual in an unhealthy, unbalanced way, but clearly God wants us to know about this coming prince of darkness, for He has chosen to tell us a lot about him. The sheer volume of information about the Antichrist in Scripture is reason enough for us to understand who he is and what he will do.

Second, knowing about what will happen to the Antichrist gives us confidence that God will ultimately triumph over all evil. If God is certain to have victory over the greatest human concentration of evil ever in the person known as Antichrist, then we can rest assured that He will triumph over all the evil that is running rampant in our world. This knowledge can serve as a tremendous source of comfort and reassurance in our increasingly troubled times. As Bible teacher John MacArthur said in reference to Revelation 13 and the Antichrist, "The message of this passage is clear. Let the monstrous beast from the abyss do his worst. Let

Satan and his demon hosts have their hour. God controls the future and believers belong to Him."[9]

Third, knowing about the Antichrist helps us see how current events all around us are working together to set the stage for his coming. We will look at this further when we focus on some of the signs of the Antichrist's coming. As we witness world events shaping up in the way the Bible predicted they would, we will know great peace because we will experience the assurance that comes from realizing the Bible has foretold the future with perfect accuracy.

Fourth, knowing the truth about the Antichrist can help us recognize error and apostasy in our own day. While we don't yet live in the end times, as we draw nearer to them, we can expect a growing flood of apostasy and false teaching. Prophecy teachers Thomas Ice and Timothy Demy provide this practical word:

> Biblical teaching regarding the Antichrist is not given to make us anxious, but to make us aware. Awareness of God's victory over Antichrist and all evil gives assurance to believers that both the present and the future are firmly in the grasp of God. We should be concerned about the Antichrist, not just because the Bible speaks of him or out of curiosity, but because he provides insight into the mystery of lawlessness that is already at work (2 Thessalonians 2:7). The pattern of evil which will be clearly played out in the future and personified in the Antichrist should be our concern, so that we can skillfully resist evil in the present. Even though a biblical passage or subject may not directly apply to a particular believer today, a thorough knowledge of Scripture gives the saint of God added insight in living faithfully for the Savior.[10]

God's revelation about the final embodiment of evil is another part of His message to man, and we should not dismiss or disregard it. God wants us to know about the coming Antichrist, and every believer should understand God's revelation about him as part of his or her overall understanding of God's Word and His plan for the ages.

Where does the Bible tell about the Antichrist?

The truth about the final world ruler is scattered throughout Scripture yet paints a very consistent composite of his person and work. The portrait of the Antichrist is derived from many Bible passages. I have provided some of the key ones below, and you will find it helpful to read these passages at this point because you will find them cited many times throughout the rest of this book.

Daniel 7:8

> While I was contemplating the horns, behold, another horn, a little one, came up among them, and three of the first horns were pulled out by the roots before it; and behold, this horn possessed eyes like the eyes of a man and a mouth uttering great boasts.

Daniel 8:23-25

> In the latter period of their rule, when the transgressors have run their course, a king will arise, insolent and skilled in intrigue. His power will be mighty, but not by his own power, and he will destroy to an extraordinary degree and prosper and perform his will; he will destroy mighty men and the holy people. And through his shrewdness he will cause deceit to succeed by his influence; and he will magnify himself in his heart, and he will destroy many while

they are at ease. He will even oppose the Prince of princes, but he will be broken without human agency.

Daniel 9:26-27

After the sixty-two weeks the Messiah will be cut off and have nothing, and the people of the prince who is to come will destroy the city and the sanctuary. And its end will come with a flood; even to the end there will be war; desolations are determined.

And he will make a firm covenant with the many for one week, but in the middle of the week he will put a stop to sacrifice and grain offering; and on the wing of abominations will come one who makes desolate, even until a complete destruction, one that is decreed, is poured out on the one who makes desolate.

Daniel 11:36-39

The king will do as he pleases, and he will exalt and magnify himself above every god and will speak monstrous things against the God of gods; and he will prosper until the indignation is finished, for that which is decreed will be done. He will show no regard for the gods of his fathers or for the desire of women, nor will he show regard for any other god; for he will magnify himself above them all. But instead he will honor a god of fortresses, a god whom his fathers did not know; he will honor him with gold, silver, costly stones and treasures. He will take action against the strongest of fortresses with the help of a foreign god; he will give great honor to those who acknowledge him and will cause them to rule over the many, and will parcel out land for a price.

Matthew 24:23-24

If anyone says to you, "Behold, here is the Christ," or "There He is," do not believe him. For false Christs and false prophets will arise and will show great signs and wonders, so as to mislead, if possible, even the elect.

2 Thessalonians 2:3-8

Let no one in any way deceive you, for it will not come unless the apostasy comes first, and the man of lawlessness is revealed, the son of destruction, who opposes and exalts himself above every so-called god or object of worship, so that he takes his seat in the temple of God, displaying himself as being God. Do you not remember that while I was still with you, I was telling you these things? And you know what restrains him now, so that in his time he will be revealed. For the mystery of lawlessness is already at work; only he who now restrains will do so until he is taken out of the way. Then that lawless one will be revealed whom the Lord will slay with the breath of His mouth and bring to an end by the appearance of His coming; that is, the one whose coming is in accord with the activity of Satan, with all power and signs and false wonders.

The only places in the New Testament where the term "Antichrist" appears are in 1 John 2:18,22; 4:3; and 2 John 7.

1 John 2:18,22

Children, it is the last hour; and just as you heard that antichrist is coming, even now many antichrists have appeared; from this we know that it is the last hour...Who is the liar but the one who denies that Jesus is the Christ?

This is the antichrist, the one who denies the Father and the Son.

1 John 4:1-3

Beloved, do not believe every spirit, but test the spirits to see whether they are from God, because many false prophets have gone out into the world. By this you know the Spirit of God: every spirit that confesses that Jesus Christ has come in the flesh is from God; and every spirit that does not confess Jesus is not from God; this is the spirit of the antichrist, of which you have heard that it is coming, and now it is already in the world.

2 John 7

Many deceivers have gone out into the world, those who do not acknowledge Jesus Christ as coming in the flesh. This is the deceiver and the antichrist.

The final main passages that deal with the coming Antichrist are found in the book of Revelation.

Revelation 13:1-10

The dragon stood on the sand of the seashore.
Then I saw a beast coming up out of the sea, having ten horns and seven heads, and on his horns were ten diadems, and on his heads were blasphemous names. And the beast which I saw was like a leopard, and his feet were like those of a bear, and his mouth like the mouth of a lion. And the dragon gave him his power and his throne and great authority. I saw one of his heads as if it

had been slain, and his fatal wound was healed. And the whole earth was amazed and followed after the beast; they worshiped the dragon because he gave his authority to the beast; and they worshiped the beast, saying, "Who is like the beast, and who is able to wage war with him?" There was given to him a mouth speaking arrogant words and blasphemies, and authority to act for forty-two months was given to him. And he opened his mouth in blasphemies against God, to blaspheme His name and His tabernacle, that is, those who dwell in heaven.

It was also given to him to make war with the saints and to overcome them, and authority over every tribe and people and tongue and nation was given to him. All who dwell on the earth will worship him, everyone whose name has not been written from the foundation of the world in the book of life of the Lamb who has been slain. If anyone has an ear, let him hear. If anyone is destined for captivity, to captivity he goes; if anyone kills with the sword, with the sword he must be killed. Here is the perseverance and the faith of the saints.

Revelation 17:9-17

Here is the mind which has wisdom. The seven heads are seven mountains on which the woman sits, and they are seven kings; five have fallen, one is, the other has not yet come; and when he comes, he must remain a little while. The beast which was and is not, is himself also an eighth and is one of the seven, and he goes to destruction. The ten horns which you saw are ten kings who have not yet received a kingdom, but they receive authority as kings with the beast for one hour. These have one purpose, and they give their power and authority to the beast. These will wage war against the Lamb, and the Lamb will overcome them, because He is Lord of lords and King of kings, and those who are with Him are the called and chosen and faithful.

And he said to me, "The waters which you saw where the harlot sits, are peoples and multitudes and nations and tongues. And the ten horns which you saw, and the beast, these will hate the harlot and will make her desolate and naked, and will eat her flesh and will burn her up with fire. For God has put it in their hearts to execute His purpose by having a common purpose, and by giving their kingdom to the beast, until the words of God will be fulfilled."

With this biblical foundation in mind, let's move forward and see what some of the early church fathers believed about the rise of Antichrist.

What did the early church believe about him?

There's a growing chorus of voices that maintain that the view of a future individual who will rule the world is a modern invention. Gary DeMar, who represents this view and criticizes Bible teacher and author Tim LaHaye and the Left Behind series, says that the idea of a final Antichrist is "modern." To him it's just a myth. He repeatedly refers to the Left Behind view of the Antichrist as "the modern Antichrist doctrine," "LaHaye's modern Antichrist doctrine," and "the modern doctrine of the Antichrist as outlined by LaHaye and many other prophecy writers."[11]

But is this view of the Antichrist a myth? Or is it a recent invention? The evidence reveals that it goes all the way back to the earliest days of the church. Of course, the interpretations of early church fathers do not prove the truth of this view per se, but they do provide a historical backdrop for the view of a final, future Antichrist and they certainly demonstrate that this position has been around for a very long time.

For example, the *Didache* or Teaching of the Twelve Apostles was written sometime between AD 70–100. This early church document recognized the coming of a personal Antichrist who would bring a time of unparalleled trouble on the earth.

> For as lawlessness increases, they will hate and perse-
> cute and betray one another. And then the deceiver of
> the world will appear as a son of God and "will perform
> signs and wonders, and the earth will be delivered into
> his hands, and he will commit abominations the likes of
> which have never happened before."[12]

Irenaeus, the bishop of Lyons in France, probably had more influence than any other Christian leader in the first three centuries. He was the first great systematic theologian of the church and a tireless defender of the faith against the surging inroads of heresy, especially Gnosticism. He included a treatment on the Antichrist in his great work *Against Heresies.* In that work he detailed his view of the coming evil one. At one point he concludes:

> …when this Antichrist shall have devastated all things in
> this world, he will reign for three years and six months,
> and sit in the temple at Jerusalem; and then the Lord
> will come from heaven in the clouds, in the glory of the
> Father, sending this man and those who follow him into
> the lake of fire; but bringing in for the righteous the times
> of the kingdom, that is, the rest, the hallowed seventh

day; and restoring to Abraham the promised inheritance, in which kingdom the Lord declared, that many coming from the east and from the west should sit down with Abraham, Isaac, and Jacob (*Against Heresies* 5.30.4).

From this we can safely say that Irenaeus believed the following about the coming world ruler:

- Antichrist is a single individual whose coming was still future in the second century AD.
- He will totally embody evil just as Christ does good.[13]
- He will lead the final great apostasy (5.21.1; 5.28.2).
- He will be promoted by the false prophet, who will perform great miracles that will lead many people astray (5.28.2).
- He will rise from the "last kingdom" when ten kings are ruling the Roman Empire (5.25.3; 5.30.2).
- He will be a Jew from the tribe of Dan.[14]
- He will sit in the temple of God and declare himself to be God (5.25.2; 5.28.2).
- He will reign over the world for a period of three-and-a-half years.[15]
- Then the Lord will cast him into the lake of fire (5.28.2).

Irenaeus, a luminary in the second century, held a view about the Antichrist that is very similar to what is being presented in this book and by many other modern-day prophecy teachers.

Moving along to the third century, Hippolytus was presbyter of Rome from about AD 200–235. He wrote the earliest surviving, complete Christian biblical commentary, titled *Commentary on Daniel*. It was written around AD 204. He also penned an entire treatise concerning Antichrist called *On Christ and the Antichrist*. Hippolytus listed six ways in which Antichrist will be a perverted imitation of Christ: (1) He will be of Jewish origin; (2) he will send out apostles; (3) he will bring together people who are spread abroad; (4) he will seal his followers; (5) he will appear in the form of a man; and (6) he will build a temple in Jerusalem.[16] He also taught that Antichrist would rise from a ten-kingdom form of the Roman Empire, that he would rebuild the Roman Empire, that his career would last for three-and-a-half years, and that he would persecute Christians who refuse to worship him.[17] Hippolytus especially noted the Jewish connection of the Antichrist. "Above all, moreover, he will love the nation of the Jews. And with all these [Jews] he will work signs and terrible wonders, false wonders and not true, in order to deceive his impious equals…And after that he will build the temple in Jerusalem and will restore it again speedily and give it over to the Jews" (Hippolytus, *Discourse on the End of the World* 23-25).

Tertullian was the first major voice in Latin Christianity, and he lived from about AD 160–220. In his work *Against Marcion* he said,

> [T]he man of sin, the son of perdition, who must first be revealed before the Lord comes, who opposes and exalts himself above all that is called God or that is worshipped; and who is to sit in the temple of God and boast himself as being God… According indeed to our view, he is Antichrist; as it is taught us in both the ancient and the new prophecies, and by the apostle John, who says that "already many false prophets have gone out into the world," the forerunners of Antichrist, who deny that Christ is come in the flesh, and do not acknowledge Jesus, meaning in God the Creator (*Against Marcion* 5:16 [AD 210]).

Tertullian made it clear that he believed both in present "antichrists" who were heretics who divided the church, and also in a coming final Antichrist who will persecute God's people.[18]

Cyrpian of Carthage, in about AD 250 wrote that he believed Antichrist was a future individual who would rise as a great persecutor of God's people (*Letters* 69[70]:3).

Cyril, bishop of Jerusalem, lived from about AD 315–386. Based on Daniel 7:13-27, 2 Thessalonians 2:4, and other passages commonly related to Antichrist, Cyril expected a single future Antichrist who will be a powerful, skilled worker of magic and sorcery. He will be the eleventh king of the fragmented Roman Empire and will rebuild the destroyed Jewish temple and enthrone himself there as god.[19]

Lactantius, who became an advisor to the first Christian Roman emperor, Constantine, also wrote about the future Antichrist in the early fourth century:

> [A] king shall arise out of Syria, born from an evil spirit, the overthrower and destroyer of the human race, who shall destroy that which is left by the former evil, together with himself…But that king will not only be most disgraceful in himself, but he will also be a prophet of lies, and he will constitute and call himself God, and will order himself to be worshipped as the Son of God, and power will be given to him to do signs and wonders, by the sight of which he may entice men to adore him. He will command fire to come down from heaven and the sun to stand and leave his course, and an image to speak, and these things shall be done at his word…Then he will attempt to destroy the temple of God and persecute the righteous people (*Divine Institutes* 7:17).

Jerome (AD 331–420), the great Latin father of the church who translated the Scriptures into Latin, also believed in a personal Antichrist. He too believed Antichrist would be a Jew, but he also held that he would be born of a virgin and indwelt by Satan himself. He further taught that the Roman Empire would be partitioned by ten kings who would be overcome by Antichrist, the eleventh king. He said the Antichrist would die on the Mount of Olives, the same place where Christ ascended to heaven.[20]

Even the great Augustine, in the early fifth century, held to the idea of a future Antichrist. He said,

> Daniel prophesies of the last judgment in such a way as to indicate that Antichrist shall first come and to carry on his destruction to the eternal reign of the saints. For when in prophetic vision he had seen four beasts, signifying four kingdoms, and the fourth conquered by a certain king, who is recognized as Antichrist, and after this the eternal kingdom of the Son of Man, that is to say, of Christ (*The City of God* 20:19).

Bernard McGinn, a noted expert on the Antichrist, quotes David Dunbar, a renowned patristic scholar, who says that a "kind of mainline eschatology" had developed that was

> quite widespread during the closing decades of the second century. This mainline view in the church was that Antichrist would be a future Jewish individual from the tribe of Dan; he will come after the fragmentation of the Roman empire; he will be a persecuting tyrant; he will rebuild the temple in Jerusalem; he will exalt himself as god; he will rule for three and a half years; his fall will usher in Christ's return to earth.[21]

McGinn concludes with a challenge to modern teachers who reject the biblical truth about the Antichrist. He says, "These Christian fathers still offer food for thought to those at the end of the twentieth century who have lost belief in any literal Final Opponent."[22]

Kim Riddlebarger, an amillennial scholar and pastor, observes, "The church fathers, by and large, believed that the Antichrist would be an apostate Jew who would appear after the fall of the Roman Empire and who would claim to be the Messiah in a rebuilt temple in Jerusalem."[23]

This same general picture of the Antichrist continued on into the Middle Ages. In his book *Naming the Antichrist,* Robert Fuller summarizes the dominant medieval view of the Antichrist:

> Although the medieval Antichrist tradition was very complex and varied from author to author, it is nonetheless possible to discern a standard and widely accepted medieval understanding of the Antichrist: who he is, when he will appear, what he will do, and what will become of him...The medieval tradition wavered somewhat between identifying contemporary heretics (especially Jews) as antichrists and expecting a single, specific individual who would come in the future immediately before the return of Christ. On the whole, the latter interpretation was the dominant one, and medieval clergy wrote at length about a man who would be born of a whore or some other evil woman, of Jewish parentage from the tribe of Dan. It was thought that from his birth onward, he would be possessed by the devil, who would instruct him in the powers of deception and wonder making. The various "lives of the Antichist" state that he will enter Jerusalem, rebuild the temple, and convert the Jews, who will initially embrace him as their ally.

He will gain political and religious power, send out false prophets, destroy belief in Jesus as the Son of God, and institute a new law. This master of deceit will appear to perform miracles and will demand to be worshiped as God. When the biblical prophets Enoch and Elias appear to challenge his rule and convert Jews to the true Christ, he will kill them and persecute their followers. In his final parody of Christ, the Antichrist will attempt to rise to heaven from the Mount of Olives. At or about this moment Christ will return from the heavens, destroy the Antichrist "with the spirit of his mouth," and inaugurate the millennial period as described in Revelation.[24]

As you can see, this view of the Antichrist from the earliest days of church history on through the Middle Ages strikingly resembles the modern, futurist view of the Antichrist. The view that he will be an individual who will rise in the end times is almost a mirror image of the view of the early church fathers and medieval clergy. This view, far from being modern, or being a myth, dates back to the ancient church and comes from those who were closest in time to the New Testament and the apostles. Some people may disagree with the idea of a great Antichrist in the last days, but claiming that such a view is of recent vintage is not at all accurate.

Will believers know who the Antichrist is before the rapture? Should we to try to figure out his identity?

The identity of Antichrist has intrigued people for 2000 years. As we noted earlier, many have found it difficult to resist the temptation to identify the Antichrist. Nevertheless, as alluring as it may be at times to try to point out who the man of sin is, we must avoid attempting to do so. Those who have given in to this temptation often draw a great deal of attention for a while, but when they are eventually proven wrong, they highlight the danger of trying to specifically identify the Antichrist before the proper time.

Many who try to identify the Antichrist make use of the number 666 in Revelation 13:16-18 in one way or another. We will discuss 666—or the mark of the beast—in more detail later. For now it suffices to say that many speculators attempt to apply the number to the names of current candidates in order to come up with a correlation. G. Salmon, a biblical scholar, has observed three "strategies" people have used throughout the centuries in their attempts to identify the Antichrist and make certain names equal to the number 666:

> Rule #1—If the person's name doesn't equal 666, throw in a title.
>
> Rule #2—If you can't get the name to add up in English, try Greek or Hebrew, or even Latin.
>
> Rule #3—Don't be too particular about how the name is spelled.

With enough ingenuity, then, a person can make almost anyone out to be the Antichrist. As Salmon concludes, "We cannot infer too much from the fact that a key fits the lock if it is a lock in which almost any key will turn."[25]

But this has not stopped people from playing "pin the tail on the Antichrist." That raises the following questions: Is it even possible for us to know the identity of the Antichrist in this age? Should we even take the time to try to figure out who he is?

There is a key passage in the New Testament—2 Thessalonians

2:1-8—that many Bible teachers read as saying that the rapture must come before the revelation of Antichrist. In other words, it is not possible to know who the Antichrist is before Christians are raptured to heaven. This means that Revelation 13:16-18 speaks to those believers who are present on the earth *after* the rapture. The passage provides information that will enable them to figure out who he is when he rises on the scene. Let's look briefly at 2 Thessalonians 2:1-8 and see what it teaches us about the relationship between the rapture and the appearance of Antichrist.

The Day of the Lord

In 2 Thessalonians, Paul wrote to the Thessalonian believers in northern Greece to clear up some confusion they had about the coming day of the Lord (which I believe begins with the seven-year Tribulation). Evidently someone had taught the Thessalonian believers that they were already in the Tribulation. Paul corrected this error by pointing out that the day of the Lord can't come until two things happen: (1) a great apostasy or rebellion, and (2) the revelation of the Antichrist or man of lawlessness.

Second Thessalonians 2:1-3 says,

> Now we request you, brethren, with regard to the coming of our Lord Jesus Christ and our gathering together to Him, that you not be quickly shaken from your composure or be disturbed either by a spirit or a message or a letter as if from us, to the effect that the day of the Lord has come. Let no one in any way deceive you, for it will not come unless the apostasy comes first, and the man of lawlessness is revealed, the son of destruction.

Since, as many Bible teachers believe, the Antichrist will be revealed at the beginning of the Day of the Lord (the Tribulation period), and the church will be raptured before this time, it doesn't appear that we who are Christians will know the identity of the Antichrist before we are taken to heaven. If you ever do figure out who the Antichrist is, then I've got bad news for you: You've been left behind!

Sometime after the rapture, the Antichrist will come on the scene to sign a peace covenant with Israel, and then the Tribulation will begin. No doubt the chaos and confusion created by the disappearance of millions of people worldwide at the rapture will make the environment ripe for the Antichrist to quickly rise to global prominence. The world will be desperate for answers, for solutions, for someone who can bring order. The Antichrist will catapult onto the scene with answers and many will be enamored with him, but the honeymoon won't last long because the world will face seven years of terrible tribulation.

The Removal of the Restrainer

There is another way in which the apostle Paul made a connection between the rapture and the Antichrist in 2 Thessalonians 2. He said the Antichrist cannot be revealed until "he who now restrains" is taken out of the way. This restrainer is referred to both as a person and a power.

> Let no one in any way deceive you, for it will not come unless the apostasy comes first, and the man of lawlessness is revealed, the son of destruction, who opposes and exalts himself above every so-called god or object of worship, so that he takes his seat in the temple of God, displaying himself as being God. Do you not remember that while I was still with you, I was telling you these things? And you know what restrains him now, so that

in his time he will be revealed, for the mystery of lawlessness is already at work; only he who now restrains will do
so until he is taken out of the way. Then that lawless one
will be revealed whom the Lord will slay with the breath
of His mouth and bring to an end by the appearance of
His coming (2 Thessalonians 2:2-8).

God is telling us there is a specific obstacle that is hindering
the full outbreak of evil and the opening of the door for Antichrist's entrance onto the world stage. And this hindrance is called
"he who now restrains." While there are many explanations given
with regard to the identity of the restrainer, I believe the view that
makes the most sense is that the restrainer is the Holy Spirit working in and through the church, the body of Christ on earth.[26]

There are four reasons for identifying the one who "holds
back" the Antichrist as the restraining ministry of the Holy Spirit
through the church:

1. This restraint requires omnipotent power. The only one
   with the power to restrain and hold back the appearance of Antichrist is God.

2. This is the only view that adequately explains the change
   in gender in 2 Thessalonians 2:6-7. The restrainer is
   both a power—"what restrains him now," and a person—"he who now restrains." In the original Greek
   text, the word *pneuma* (Spirit) is neuter. But in Scripture, the Holy Spirit is also consistently referred to by
   the masculine pronoun "He," especially in John 14–16.

3. The Holy Spirit is spoken of in Scripture as restraining
   sin and evil in the world (Genesis 6:3) and in the heart
   of the believer (Galatians 5:16-17).

4. The church and its mission of proclaiming and portraying the gospel is the primary instrument the Holy Spirit uses to restrain evil in this age. We are the salt of the earth and the light of the world (Matthew 5:13-16). We are the temple of the Holy Spirit both individually and corporately.

The restrainer, then, is the restraining influence and ministry of the Holy Spirit, which occurs as He indwells and works through His people. I love how the well-known Bible teacher Donald Grey Barnhouse describes the identity of the restrainer:

> Well, what is keeping the Antichrist from putting in his appearance on the world stage? *You* are! You and every other member of the body of Christ on earth. The presence of the church of Jesus Christ is the restraining force that refuses to allow the man of lawlessness to be revealed. True, it is the Holy Spirit who is the real restrainer. But as both 1 Corinthians 3:16 and 6:19 teach, the Holy Spirit indwells the believer. The believer's body is the temple of the Spirit of God. Put all believers together, then, with the Holy Spirit indwelling each of us, and you have a formidable restraining force.
>
> For when the church is removed at the rapture, the Holy Spirit goes with the church insofar as His restraining power is concerned. His work in this age of grace will be ended. Henceforth, during the Great Tribulation, the Holy Spirit will still be here on earth, of course—for how can you get rid of God?—but He will not be indwelling believers as He does now. Rather, He will revert to His Old Testament ministry of "coming upon" special people.[27]

When the rapture occurs, the Spirit-indwelt church and its

restraining influence will be removed from the earth. Satan will then be able to put his plan into full swing by bringing his man onto center stage to take control of the world. The rapture will throw the door wide open for the Antichrist to come to power and bring forth an outbreak of evil unlike any that has ever occurred before. The fact the restrainer is still in place right now means that Satan must wait on God's timing before he can unveil the Antichrist. That God is sovereign in this way also assures us that Satan's eventual defeat is certain long before he ever even begins his last-days assault on God and His people. He can't make his final diabolical move until God releases him to do so by removing the restraining power of the Spirit in the church.[28]

Looking for Christ

We must remember this important fact: The Antichrist will not be revealed until after the church is taken to heaven. That's why no one can know the identity of the Antichrist until all believers are raptured. We should follow the advice of Irenaeus when it comes to attempts to identify the Antichrist:

> It is therefore more certain, and less hazardous, to await the fulfilment of the prophecy, than to be making surmises, and casting about for any names that may present themselves, inasmuch as many names can be found possessing the number mentioned; and the same question will, after all, remain unsolved. For if there are many names found possessing this number, it will be asked which among them shall the coming man bear (*Against Heresies* 5.30.3).

This also explains why believers are never told to look for Antichrist but for Christ. We will meet the Lord in the air before the man of sin is unveiled and begins his nefarious career. We are looking for the One whose name is above every name, the One before whom every knee will bow and every tongue will confess that He is Lord, to the glory of God the Father (Philippians 2:9-11).

PART 2

The Character of the Antichrist

——◯——

*"Across the varied scenes depicted by prophecy
there falls the shadow of a figure at once
commanding and ominous. Under many
different names, like the aliases of a criminal, his
character and movements are set before us."*

A.W. PINK, *THE ANTICHRIST* (1923)

What does the word *Antichrist* mean?

Before we go any further in our discussion of the Antichrist, it's important that we pause briefly to make sure we know exactly who it is we are talking about. The prefix *anti* can mean "against, opposed to" or "instead of, in place of." This raises a key question: Will this future Antichrist be "against" Christ, or "in place of" Christ? That is, should we understand the prefix *anti* to refer to opposition or an exchange? Will the Antichrist be a counterfeit Messiah, or will he simply work against Christ Himself?

Both of these meanings are undoubtedly included in the term *Anti*christ. He will be the archenemy and the ultimate opponent of the Lord Jesus. The origins, natures, and purposes of Christ and the Antichrist are diametrically opposed. This list of titles reveals the gaping chasm that is present between Christ and His adversary.[1]

Christ	Antichrist
The Truth	The Lie
The Holy One	The Lawless One
The Man of Sorrows	The Man of Sin
The Son of God	The Son of Destruction
The Mystery of Godliness	The Mystery of Iniquity
Cleanses the Temple	Desecrates the Temple
The Lamb	The Beast

The total opposition of Antichrist to Christ is seen in these contrasting descriptions.[2]

Feature:	Christ	Antichrist
Origin:	Heaven	Bottomless pit
Nature:	The Good Shepherd	The foolish shepherd
Destiny:	To be exalted on high	To be cast down into hell
Goal:	To do His Father's will	To do his own will
Purpose:	To save the lost	To destroy the holy people
Authority:	His Father's name	His own name
Attitude:	Humbled Himself	Will exalt himself
Fruit:	The true vine	The vine of the earth
Response:	Despised	Admired

In every way that could be imagined, Christ and Antichrist are fundamentally opposed. The Antichrist is contrary to Christ, and he will be anti- (against) Christ.

The Antichrist will not only be anti Christ in the sense he is against Christ; he will also be anti Christ in the sense of trying to put himself "in place of" Christ. He will be an amazing parody or counterfeit of the true Christ. He will be a substitute Christ, a mock Christ, a pseudo Christ, an imitation Christ.

In John 5:43, Jesus said, "I have come in My Father's name, and you do not receive Me; if another shall come in his own name, you will receive him." The one coming in his own name will be the world's final false Messiah, the Antichrist. He will attempt to be the alter ego of the true Christ. A.W. Pink said,

> At every point he is the antithesis of Christ. The word "Antichrist" has a double significance. Its primary meaning is one who is opposed to Christ; but its secondary meaning is one who is instead of Christ...Not only does *anti*-christ denote the antagonism of Christ, but tells of one who is instead of Christ. The word signifies another Christ, a pro-Christ, an alter christus, a pretender to the name of Christ. He will seem to be and will set himself up as the true Christ. He will be the Devil's counterfeit.[3]

As has often been pointed out, Satan has never originated anything except sin. From the time of creation he has counterfeited the works of God. Antichrist is no exception. He is Satan's ultimate masterpiece—the crowning counterfeit—a false Christ and forged replica of Jesus, the true Christ and Son of God.

Here are 20 ways Antichrist will mimic the ministry of the true Son of God.

Christ	Antichrist
Miracles, signs, and wonders (Matthew 9:32-33; Mark 6:2)	Miracles, signs, and wonders (Matthew 24:24; 2 Thessalonians 2:9)
Appears in the millennial temple (Ezekiel 43:6-7)	Sits in the Tribulation temple (2 Thessalonians 2:4)
Is God (John 1:1-2; 10:35)	Claims to be God (2 Thessalonians 2:4)
Is the Lion from Judah (Revelation 5:5)	Has a mouth like a lion (Revelation 13:2)
Makes a peace covenant with Israel (Ezekiel 37:26)	Makes a peace covenant with Israel (Daniel 9:27)
Causes men to worship God (Revelation 1:6)	Causes men to worship Satan (Revelation 13:3-4)
Followers sealed on their forehead (Revelation 7:4; 14:1)	Followers sealed on their forehead or right hand (Revelation 13:16-18)
Worthy name (Revelation 19:16)	Blasphemous names (Revelation 13:1)
Married to a virtuous bride (Revelation 19:7-10)	Married to a vile prostitute (Revelation 17:3-5)
Crowned with many crowns (Revelation 19:12)	Crowned with ten crowns (Revelation 13:1)
Is *the* King of kings (Revelation 19:16)	Is called "the king" (Daniel 11:36)
Sits on a throne (Revelation 3:21; 12:5; 20:11)	Sits on a throne (Revelation 13:2; 16:10)
Sharp sword from His mouth (Revelation 19:15)	Bow in his hand (Revelation 6:2)

Rides a white horse (Revelation 19:11)	Rides a white horse (Revelation 6:2)
Has an army (Revelation 19:14)	Has an army (Revelation 6:2; 19:19)
Violent death (Revelation 5:6; 13:8)	Violent death (Revelation 13:3)
Resurrection (Matthew 28:6)	Resurrection (Revelation 13:3,14)
Second coming (Revelation 19:11-21)	Second coming (Revelation 17:8)
1000-year worldwide kingdom (Revelation 20:1-6)	3½-year worldwide kingdom (Revelation 13:5-8)
Part of a holy Trinity (Father, Son, and Holy Spirit—2 Corinthians 13:14)	Part of an unholy trinity (Satan, Antichrist, and the false prophet—Revelation 13)

One New Testament passage that highlights the ways Antichrist will counterfeit the true Christ is 2 Thessalonians 2:3-8. The Greek words translated "power," "signs," and "wonders" used to describe the deceiving miracles of Antichrist are the very same Greek words used in the Gospels to describe the genuine miracles of Christ. Also, the words translated "revealed" (*apokalupsis*) and "coming" (*parousia*) that are used to describe the explosion of the Antichrist on the world scene are the same Greek words used to describe the second coming of Jesus Christ. J. Dwight Pentecost aptly summarizes the biblical meaning of the word *Antichrist:* "Satan is seeking to give the world a ruler in place of Christ who will also be in opposition to Christ so that he can rule over the world, instead of Christ."[4]

Will the Antichrist be an actual, individual person?

Because the title *Antichrist* is the one that most people are familiar with today, it's important that we know something about the meaning of this word. "Antichrist" or "antichrists" (Greek = *antichristos*) is found only five times in the New Testament. All five instances appear in the epistles of John (twice in 1 John 2:18; and once each in 1 John 2:22; 4:3; 2 John 7).

> Children, it is the last hour; and just as you have heard that antichrist is coming, even now many antichrists have appeared; from this we know that it is the last hour (1 John 2:18).

> Who is the liar but the one who denies that Jesus is the Christ? This is the antichrist, the one who denies the Father and the Son (1 John 2:22).

> Every spirit that does not confess Jesus is not from God; this is the spirit of the antichrist, of which you have heard that it is coming, and now it is already in the world (1 John 4:3).

> Many deceivers have gone out into the world, those who do not acknowledge Jesus Christ as coming in the flesh. This is the deceiver and the antichrist (2 John 7).

Note how John opened 1 John 2:18: "Children, it is the last hour; and just as you have heard…antichrist is coming." John's readers knew about the coming future Antichrist. The title "antichrist" might have been new to them, but the fact of his coming was not. John had undoubtedly taught them about the Antichrist, and they had likely read about his coming in the Old Testament in books such as Daniel. Years earlier, when the apostle

Paul was in Ephesus, he had also taught these same believers what John was now addressing in his letters. These Christians clearly had heard about the coming of this final great deceiver just as the Thessalonian believers had heard about him from Paul (2 Thessalonians 2:1-12).[5]

John's purpose was to warn his fellow believers about present-day false teachers who came in the spirit of Antichrist and displayed hostility toward the true Christ. In the epistles John wrote, he was primarily concerned with the doctrinal error of denying the person of Jesus Christ. John stated that even in his own day many "antichrists" (false teachers) had appeared who were denying the true Christ and deceiving many. And those antichrists were among the first to promote the antichrist philosophy that Satan that was already at work advocating (1 John 4:3; 2 Thessalonians 2:7).

Today, the number of people who deny a future, individual Antichrist is growing. Hank Hanegraaff, president of CRI (Christian Research Institute), represents this view and denies the notion of a future, individual Antichrist. He says, "John did not reserve the title 'Antichrist' for any one particular individual; rather, he taught that anyone who denies the incarnation, messianic role or deity of Jesus is the Antichrist."[6]

Preterist Gary DeMar supports this same idea and says this: "Not one of John's statements relates to the modern doctrine of the Antichrist as outlined by LaHaye and many other prophecy writers."[7] He adds, "According to the Bible, Antichrist is not a single individual."[8] He also says, "Yet one cannot reach this conclusion by studying John's biblical description of Antichrist."[9]

These dogmatic assertions that John's statements cannot be understood as referring to an individual, personal Antichrist are contrary to what John actually wrote in the Bible. Notice in 1 John 2:18 that John referred to an "antichrist" (*antichristos,* singular) who is coming in the future, and to "antichrists" (*antichristoi,* plural) who are already present.[10] John's use of the singular form when speaking of the Antichrist stands in stark contrast to the plural "antichrists" and clearly denotes that he is pointing to a specific individual. By using both the singular and the plural forms in 1 John 2:18, John taught about the plural antichrists and false teachers of his day who embodied the denying, deceiving spirit of the singular future Antichrist. The plural antichrists were forerunners of the singular Antichrist and served as powerful evidence that his spirit was already at work in the world.[11]

Bible teacher and commentator James Montgomery Boice is representative of this almost universal view. Boice said, "[John] is saying that the spirit that will characterize the final antichrist is already working in those who have recently left his readers' congregations. The future antichrist will be a substitute for Christ, as much like Jesus as possible for a tool of Satan to be."[12] The renowned New Testament scholar F.F. Bruce agrees. "So it was with John. That Antichrist would come he and his readers knew, and in the false teachers he discerned the agents, or at least the forerunners, of Antichrist, sharing his nature so completely that they could be called 'many antichrists.'"[13] Kim Riddlebarger supports this consensus view:

> I believe that the church has faced a series of antichrists from the time of the apostles and that this series of antichrists will culminate in the appearance of the Antichrist immediately before the return of Jesus Christ at the end of the age. This future appearance of Antichrist reflects the fact that he is a false Messiah *par excellence* who mimics the work of Christ. As Christ died, was raised from

the dead, and will return, so too Antichrist has his own death, resurrection, and second coming, all designed to imitate the redemption secured by Christ so as to direct worship unto his master, the dragon.[14]

In other words, John was looking beyond the many lesser antichrists (small *a*) of his own day toward the one ultimate Antichrist (capital *A*) who will culminate the manifestation of the lawless system that denies Christ and deceives men. Make no mistake. The Bible teaches that an ultimate, final, individual Antichrist is coming.

What is the "spirit" of Antichrist?

Part of the confusion about the coming Antichrist arises from the fact that the term "antichrist" in the New Testament is applied to both an individual and the evil system he represents. As we've seen, the term "antichrist" appears only five times in the New Testament, and all five are in the epistles of John.

A closer look at 1 John 4:1-3 helps to clear away some of the confusion. There we read, "Beloved, do not believe every spirit, but test the spirits to see whether they are from God, because many false prophets have gone out into the world. By this you know the Spirit of God: every spirit that confesses that Jesus Christ has come in the flesh is from God; and every spirit that does not confess Jesus is not from God; this is the spirit of the antichrist, of which you have heard that it is coming, and now it is already in the world."

According to this text, when John wrote this letter in the late first century AD, the recipients of this letter not only knew that the spirit of antichrist was coming, but also that he was "already in the world." That's why John called upon God's people to "test the spirits to see whether they are from God, because many false prophets have gone out into the world." These were the traveling false teachers in his day who did not acknowledge and confess that Jesus is from God. This gives us a clue as to the meaning of "the spirit of the antichrist." In its broadest sense "the spirit of the antichrist" is a satanically inspired and energized expression of lawlessness and rebellion against God, the things of God, and the people of God. It's the anti-Christian spirit that works feverishly to oppose, undermine, deny, twist, distort, and reject the truth about Jesus Christ.

Some believe that "the spirit of the antichrist" is actually Satan himself, who is the real person behind it all and will be the empowering force behind the final Antichrist when he rises. In either case, the spirit of Antichrist is alive and well. As prophecy teacher Ed Hindson notes, "The New Testament authors assure us that the spirit of Antichrist was active in their day over 20 centuries ago. It has remained active throughout the whole of church history, expressing itself in persecutions, heresies, spiritual deceptions, false prophets, and false religions. Satan has battled the church at every turn throughout its long history, waiting for the right moment to indwell the right person—the Antichrist—his final masterpiece."[15]

The same Antichrist "spirit" is referred to as the "mystery of lawlessness" in 2 Thessalonians 2:7, which says, "The mystery of lawlessness is already at work; only he who now restrains will do so until he is taken out of the way." The man of lawlessness in 2 Thessalonians 2:3 has not yet been revealed, but the mystery of lawlessness is in full swing. The word "mystery" in that passage (and in the New Testament) doesn't refer to something mysterious as we often think of it today, but rather to something that was previously hidden and unknown to man and has now been revealed by God (Romans 16:26; Ephesians 1:9; 3:3-5; Colossians

1:25-27). A mystery is unveiled by divine revelation. In 2 Thessalonians 2:7, the mystery is the lawlessness that the Antichrist embodies. It's his anti-law, anti-Christ, anti-God agenda. Before the sinister Antichrist is openly revealed, the spirit of lawlessness that will dominate his career will already be at work, operating secretly or "under the radar." The writers of the New Testament were convinced that the war between Christ and Antichrist had already commenced.

The antichrist spirit, the mystery of lawlessness that we see at work all around us, is just a faint foretaste of what will flood the world when the full, vicious manifestation of this spirit of rebellion against Christ erupts and is headed up by its final embodiment—the Antichrist.

What will he be like?

Revelation 12 is a key chapter in the unfolding drama of the end times. It's a highly symbolic chapter. While all of Revelation presents vivid symbols that graphically portray the characters and events of the end times, it's been pointed out that Revelation 12 is the most symbolic chapter in what is the most symbolic book in the Bible. In this chapter, Satan is depicted as a great red dragon who is cast out of heaven as the result of a great cosmic war. Revelation 12 ends by noting that "the dragon was enraged," and Revelation 13 begins by saying, "He [Satan] stood on the sand of the seashore. And I saw a beast coming up out of the sea."

The scene here is dramatic. Satan, the enraged dragon, is standing on the seashore—probably a reference to the Mediterranean Sea—calling the "beast" or Antichrist forth from the sea of the nations so Satan can embody him and bring his program for world dominion into full swing. Revelation 13 describes the coming world ruler in great detail. Much of what is revealed about the Antichrist in that chapter and Revelation 17 builds upon and amplifies what the prophet Daniel wrote about him in the Old Testament. With the help of both Daniel and Revelation, we can develop a character profile or portrait of this final world ruler. He will be one of the most powerful and popular leaders the world has ever known. A. W. Pink wrote,

> For six thousand years Satan has had full opportunity afforded him to study fallen human nature, to discover its weakest points, and to learn how to best make man do his bidding. The devil knows full well how to dazzle people by the attraction of power...He knows how to gratify the craving for knowledge...he can delight the ear with melodious music the eye with entrancing beauty... He knows how to exalt men to dizzy heights of worldly greatness and fame, and how to control that greatness so that it may be employed against God and His people.[16]

Bible commentator John Phillips gives this chilling description:

> The world will go delirious with delight at his manifestation. He will be the seeming answer to all its needs. He will be filled with all the fullness of Satan. Handsome, with a charming, rakish, devil-may-care personality, a genius, superbly at home in all the scientific disciplines, brave as a lion, and with an air of mystery about him to tease the imagination or to chill the blood as occasion may serve, a brilliant conversationalist in a score of tongues, a soul-captivating orator, he will be the idol of all mankind.[17]

Here are some of the characteristics of the Antichrist that Satan will employ to dazzle and delight the world:

1. He will be an intellectual genius (Daniel 8:23)

He will overwhelm and captivate the world with his superhuman intellect and powers of perception. Obviously, anyone who can hold the entire world under his spell and quickly convince the ten leaders of the reunited Roman Empire (the G-10) to give him complete control must have intellectual abilities that far exceed those of normal men.

2. He will be an oratorical genius (Daniel 7:8,11; 11:36; Revelation 13:5)

The whole world will be swayed by the hypnotic spell of his words. Over and over again in Bible passages about the Antichrist the focus is on his mouth that speaks great words—that is, his great speaking ability. When he talks, everyone else will listen. As A.W. Pink said,

> So it will be with this daring counterfeiter: he will have a mouth speaking very great things. He will have a perfect command and flow of language. His oratory will not only gain attention but respect. Rev. 13:2 declares that his mouth is "as the mouth of a lion" which is a symbolic expression telling of the majesty and awe-producing effects of his voice. The voice of a lion excels that of any other beast. So the Antichrist will outrival orators ancient and modern.[18]

3. He will be a political genius (Daniel 9:27; Revelation 17:11-12)

The Antichrist will emerge from relative obscurity to take the world political scene by storm. He won't make a big splash or attract much attention when he first enters the political arena. He will begin without any fanfare as a "little" horn among the ten horns in a reunited Roman Empire. He will quickly rise through the ranks and will be elected by the group of ten to rule over the reunited Roman Empire (Revelation 17:13). He will be the consummate unifier and diplomat. Everyone will love him. He will assume power under the stealth of diplomacy. His platform will be peace and prosperity. Emerging with an olive branch in his hand, he will weld opposing forces together with ease. All the dreams of the United Nations will be realized in his political policies. He will even temporarily solve the political standoff in the Middle East, which may well earn him accolades such as the Nobel Peace prize or being anointed *Time* magazine's man of the year. Daniel 9:27 reveals that he will bring such peace to the Middle East that the Temple Mount area in Jerusalem will be returned to Jewish sovereignty. He will undoubtedly be hailed as the greatest peacemaker the world has ever seen.

4. He will be an economic genius (Daniel 11:43; Revelation 13:16-17)

The Antichrist will be Satan's CEO of the world's economy. He will set interest rates, prices, stock values, and supply levels. Under his leadership, everything will be nationalized or internationalized under his personal control. With the chaos created by the rapture and the collapse of the world economy as predicted in Revelation 13:5-6, people will be willing to give all power over to one man. Much like the Germans turned to Hitler after the days of runaway inflation in Weimar Germany, the world will turn to the Antichrist in search of answers for the crushing problems the world faces. According to Revelation 13:16-17, from the midpoint of the Tribulation until the second coming of Christ, no one will be able to buy or sell without the Antichrist's permission. People all over the world will be compelled to take his mark. His one-world economy will be run by his sidekick, the false prophet. We'll meet him in the next chapter.

5. He will be a military genius (Revelation 6:2; 13:2)

At the midpoint of the Tribulation, the Antichrist's mask will come off and he will replace the olive branch with the sword. He will subjugate the whole world. All the greatness of Alexander and Napoleon will be as nothing compared to him. No one will be able to stand in the way of his conquest. He will crush everything and everyone before him. He will be the final great Caesar over the ultimate form of the Roman Empire. Some of his initial military expansion and unstoppable success is described in Daniel 11:40-44:

> At the end time the king of the South will collide with him, and the king of the North will storm against him with chariots, with horsemen and with many ships; and he will enter countries, overflow them and pass through. He will also enter the Beautiful Land, and many countries will fall; but these will be rescued out of his hand: Edom, Moab and the foremost of the sons of Ammon. Then he will stretch out his hand against other countries, and the land of Egypt will not escape. But he will gain control over the hidden treasures of gold and silver and over all the precious things of Egypt; and Libyans and Ethiopians will follow at his heels. But rumors from the East and from the North will disturb him, and he will go forth with great wrath to destroy and annihilate many.

Revelation 13:4 expresses his military might succinctly. "Who is like the beast, and who is able to wage war with him?"

6. He will be a religious genius (2 Thessalonians 2:4; Revelation 13:8)

Satan's prodigy will be able to do what no other religious leader has ever done. He will do what neither Muhammed, nor Buddha, nor any pope has ever been able to do: unite the world in worship. All the religions of the world will be brought together in the worship of one man.

Just think what genius and power and deception it will take to pull that off! Religion is one of the great dividers of people. When you were little, your parents might have told you not to talk about religion or politics around other people because of the way they often have very strong feelings about those topics and are easily angered and frustrated by those who disagree with them. Religion is frequently a separator of people. But that will all change someday. And because the world is looking more and more for a great leader, a messiah, a savior to solve the profound predicaments we all face today, it will also be open to the idea of worshiping this person.

To help us better envision what the Antichrist will be like, H.L. Willmington has provided this helpful analogy with American presidents. The coming world ruler will possess...

> The leadership of a Washington and Lincoln
>
> The eloquence of a Franklin Roosevelt
>
> The charm of a Teddy Roosevelt
>
> The charisma of a Kennedy
>
> The popularity of an Ike
>
> The political savvy of a Johnson
>
> The intellect of a Jefferson[19]

John Phillips described the Antichrist in this way:

> The Antichrist will be an attractive and charismatic figure, a genius, a demon-controlled, devil-taught charmer of men. He will have answers to the horrendous problems of mankind. He will be all things to all men: a

political statesman, a social lion, a financial wizard, an intellectual giant, a religious deceiver, a masterful orator, a gifted organizer. He will be Satan's masterpiece of deception, the world's false messiah. With boundless enthusiasm the masses will follow him and readily enthrone him in their hearts as the world's savior and god.[20]

Will he be a Jew or a Gentile?

One of my friends who used to work with John MacArthur told me that years ago John gave a sermon one Sunday and taught that the Antichrist will be a Jewish person. However, during further study the next week, he changed his mind, and delivered a subsequent sermon that presented the Antichrist as a Gentile. I don't know if this story is true or not since I wasn't there, but it does highlight the fact there is a lot of persuasive discussion on both sides of this basic issue concerning the Antichrist. This is undoubtedly one of the most asked and debated questions about the coming man of sin. At the heart of this discussion is how one should interpret the prefix *anti* in the term Antichrist. If *anti* means this individual will be opposed to Christ as the ruler of Gentile world power, then he will probably be a Gentile. However, there are many who say that if *anti* means he will attempt to stand in place of Christ as a false messiah, then this makes it more likely that he will be a Jew.

As far back as the second century AD scholars were debating this issue. Irenaeus (120–202) believed that the Antichrist would be a Jew from the tribe of Dan. He based this conclusion on Jeremiah 8:16 and the fact that the tribe of Dan is omitted from the list of the tribes of Israel in Revelation 7:4-8. However, we're not told why Dan is omitted from the list of tribes. The best possible explanation for this that I'm aware of is that Dan was the first tribe to fall into idolatrous worship.[21] There are also some who think Jacob's prophecy concerning Dan (in Genesis 49:17) might provide a clue: "Dan shall be a serpent in the way, a horned snake in the path, that bites the horse's heels, so that his rider falls backward." The connection of Dan with a serpent is interpreted as somehow having something to do with Satan, and this is related to what Revelation 13 says about the Antichrist. The consistent view of the early church during the closing decades of the second century AD was that the Antichrist would be a Jewish false messiah from the tribe of Dan. This view was also held later by Jerome (AD 331–420).

Another specific Scripture passage that is often used to substantiate the view that the Antichrist is of Jewish heritage is the King James Version translation of Daniel 11:37: "Neither shall he regard the God of his fathers…" The entire argument rests on the phrase "the God of his fathers." Those who maintain that the Antichrist will be a Jew believe that his rejection of "the God of his fathers" proves his Jewishness. However, this statement could equally apply to a Gentile whose parents were followers of Christianity. Also, in 1 John 2:18-19, where the title "antichrist" appears, the term refers to apostasy from Christianity, not from Judaism. All we can discern from Daniel 11:37, then, is that the Antichrist will totally reject whatever religion his ancestors practiced.

Moreover, in most of the more recent Bible translations (including the ASV, RSV, NASB, and NIV) the word "God" (Hebrew = *elohim*) is translated in the plural form, "gods." As commentator Arnold Fruchtenbaum observes, "In the whole context, Daniel 11:36-39, the term *god* is used a total of eight times. In the Hebrew text, six of these times it is in the singular and twice in the plural, one of which is the phrase in verse 37. The very fact that the plural form of 'god' is used in a context where the singular is found in the majority of cases makes this a reference to heathen deities and not a reference to the God of Israel."[22] Moreover, in the Septuagint, which is the earliest known Greek translation of the Hebrew Old Testament, the translation reads "gods." This is consistent with the original Hebrew text.[23]

Therefore, whether you follow the KJV translation or the newer Bible translations, it is clear that the key verse used by those who believe the Antichrist will be a Jew is far from conclusive. In fact, to the contrary, the Bible teaches clearly that the coming Antichrist will be a Gentile. His Gentile origin can be discerned from four main points.

First, biblical typology points to the Gentile origin of the Antichrist. The only historical person who is specifically identified as a "type" or preview of the person and work of the Antichrist is Antiochus Epiphanes, who was a Gentile Syrian monarch in the second century BC. Antiochus has been aptly dubbed "the Old Testament Antichrist." If the type of the Antichrist is a Gentile, then it follows that he too will be a Gentile.

Second, the origin of the beast or Antichrist is symbolically described by the apostle John in Revelation 13:1: "I saw a beast rising out of the sea." The word "sea," when used symbolically in the book of Revelation and the rest of Scripture, is a reference to the Gentile nations. This is confirmed in Revelation 17:15, where we read that "the waters which you saw…are peoples and multitudes and nations and tongues." However, the use of the word "sea" could also refer to the abyss or the deep (11:7; 17:8). If this is the case, then the statement that this beast comes up out of the sea may describe his satanic, demonic origin from the underworld.

Third, the Antichrist is presented in Scripture as the final ruler of Gentile world power. His reign marks the final phase of "the times of the Gentiles" and their rule over Israel (Luke 21:24). He will sit on the throne of the final world empire, which will raise its fist in the face of God. For a Jew to rise up as the last world ruler over Gentile powers is not logical.

Fourth, among the primary activities of the Antichrist will be persecution of the Jewish people, the invasion of Israel, and the desecration of the rebuilt Jewish Temple (Daniel 7:25; 9:27; 11:41, 45; 2 Thessalonians 2:4; Revelation 11:2; 12:6; 13:7). It is highly unlikely, if not impossible, for a Jew to be the final great persecutor of his own people. Gentiles have always led the way in the persecution of the Jews.

For these reasons, I believe the Antichrist will be a Gentile.

Will he be Satan incarnate?

The Antichrist is presented in Scripture as a complete parody or counterfeit of the true Christ. He is Christ's alter ego. Because the Antichrist is such a complete parody of Christ, is it possible that he also is the product of a counterfeit "virgin birth" and that he will be the son of Satan—that he will be Satan incarnate? Some students of Bible prophecy contend that just as Christ was the product of a human mother and the Holy Spirit (the God-man) so the Antichrist will be the product of a human mother and Satan himself (the counterfeit god-man or devil-man). This was the view of Jerome in the fourth century AD. He taught that, as the counterfeit son, the Antichrist would have a supernatural origin—he would literally be Satan's son. Hollywood latched onto this idea and popularized it in such movies as *Rosemary's Baby* (1968) and *The Omen* (1976). In *Rosemary's Baby,* a Roman Catholic couple (played by Mia Farrow and John Cassavetes) make a deal with the devil. As a result, the wife eventually gives birth to Satan incarnate. The movie is dark and disturbing. Is there any biblical basis for its view of the Antichrist as Satan incarnate?

Biblical support for this notion is drawn primarily from Genesis 3:15. There, the Lord cursed the serpent and said, "I will put enmity between you and the woman, and between your seed and her seed; he shall bruise you on the head, and you shall bruise him on the heel." In this passage, the offspring of the woman is a clear reference to the coming Messiah or Deliverer who would crush the head of the serpent once and for all. But notice that there is a reference here to "your seed," or the offspring of Satan, who will be the arch-adversary of the woman's offspring. For those who hold to a supernatural origin for the Antichrist, Genesis 3:15 is seen as the first prophecy about the coming Messiah as well as the first prophecy about the Antichrist.

While it is possible the Antichrist may have a supernatural origin, it seems better to view the Antichrist not as Satan's literal son but as a man who is totally controlled by Satan. In the Bible passages that describe the Antichrist, he is consistently presented as a man. For example, in 2 Thessalonians 2:9 we read about the person and work of the coming Antichrist, "the one whose coming is in accord with the activity of Satan, with all power and signs and false wonders." The Antichrist is described as an evil man who is energized by the power of Satan to do his wicked work.

Revelation 13:4 says that the dragon (Satan) "gave his authority to the beast" (the Antichrist). That is, the Antichrist is able to do what he can do *not* because he is Satan's offspring, but because Satan energizes and empowers him as his chosen human instrument for world rule.

A man named Adso wrote a book around AD 950 called *Letter on the Origin and Life of the Antichrist.* In this work he countered the view held by many in his day that the Antichrist will be born from a virgin and contended that he will be born from the union of a human father and mother. Nevertheless, Adso maintained that the Antichrist "will be conceived wholly in sin, generated in sin, born in sin. The devil will enter the womb of his mother at the very instant of conception. He will be fostered by the power of the devil and protected in his mother's womb."

Adso's view, which is the predominant view in church history, is very consistent with the way the Antichrist is described in the Bible. Whether Satan will enter the Antichrist at the moment of conception is debatable, but the main point remains: The Antichrist will be fully human, yet totally possessed by Satan.

Will he be an individual resurrected from the past?

As we have already observed, the Antichrist is Satan's complete parody or counterfeit of the true Christ. Part of Satan's masterful work of deception will be a counterfeit of the greatest event of Christianity—the death and resurrection of Christ. There are several verses in the book of Revelation that I believe refer to the death of the Antichrist and his alleged resurrection back to life.

Revelation 13:3

> I saw one of his heads as if it had been slain, and his fatal wound was healed. And the whole earth was amazed and followed after the beast.

Revelation 13:12-14

> He exercises all the authority of the first beast in his presence. And he makes the earth and those who dwell in it to worship the first beast, whose fatal wound was healed. He performs great signs, so that he even makes fire come down out of heaven to the earth in the presence of men.

And he deceives those who dwell on the earth because of the signs which it was given him to perform in the presence of the beast, telling those who dwell on the earth to make an image to the beast who had the wound of the sword and has come to life.

Revelation 17:8

The beast that you saw was, and is not, and is about to come up out of the abyss and go to destruction. And those who dwell on the earth, whose name has not been written in the book of life from the foundation of the world, will wonder when they see the beast, that he was and is not and will come.

Many interpret those passages as saying the Antichrist will be some person from the past who will be resurrected back to life for the purpose of playing a leading role in the final drama of the ages. Bible teacher Lehman Strauss supports this notion:

Now is it possible that the Antichrist will be a man who had died and whom Satan will raise up again? Yes, it is possible. Satan's masterpiece of deception will be a clever imitation of Christ...By reading carefully Revelation 11:7; 17:8, 11, it seems that the beast goes into the place of departed spirits, and then is raised up out of that place. In Revelation 17:8 four things are said of him: "The beast that thou sawest *was*, and *is not*; and *shall ascend out of the bottomless pit*, and *go into perdition.*" This indicates quite clearly that the Antichrist has been on earth before.[24]

Many suggestions have been offered with regard to the identity of this resurrected individual. At a conference I spoke at not long ago, a man approached me and presented at length why he believes Antiochus Epiphanes will be raised back to life as the Antichrist. The Old Testament uses Antiochus as a type of the Antichrist, and it closely associates Antiochus with the abomination of desolation. This man had a number of reasons for believing Antiochus was the person responsible for the original abomination of desolation and that this act of desecration will be repeated by the Antichrist. One of his key points was that Antiochus was slain by a fatal wound—which the book of Revelation says will happen to the Antichrist. A major problem with his view, however, is that according to the Jewish historian Josephus, Antiochus died a painful death due to a terrible intestinal disease (*Antiquities of the Jews* 12.9.1). This fact is confirmed by the apocryphal book 2 Maccabees 9:5-28. The idea that Antiochus Epiphanes will be raised back to life from a mortal head wound is not confirmed by history or Scripture.

Another historical candidate that has been suggested for the resurrected Antichrist view is the Roman emperor Nero. In the early church a widely accepted theory concerning the identity of the Antichrist was the *Nero redivivus*—that is, that the Antichrist would be Nero revived or raised back to life. Nero committed suicide in AD 68, and a series of imposters pretending to be the resurrected Nero surfaced in AD 69 and 80. And in AD 88 a serious Nero imposter appeared in Parthia. However, in spite of the popularity of this theory, especially during the years right after Nero's death, there is no biblical warrant for believing that the Antichrist will be Nero brought back to life for a final curtain call.

Another popular theory is that Antichrist will be Judas Iscariot brought back from the grave.[25] There are some Bible passages that proponents point to in their attempt to support this view. Luke 22:3 says that "Satan entered into Judas who was called Iscariot." John 6:70-71 is even stronger—there, we read, "Jesus answered them, 'Did I Myself not choose you, the twelve, and yet one of you is a devil?' Now he meant Judas the son of Simon Iscariot, for he, one of the twelve, was going to betray Him." Judas is the only man Jesus ever called "a devil" (*diabolos*).

In John 17:12, our Lord referred to Judas Iscariot as "the son of perdition" or "the one doomed to destruction" (NIV). The only other place this title is used in the New Testament is in 2 Thessalonians 2:3—"the son of destruction"—in reference to the Antichrist. Acts 1:25 states that when Judas died he went "to his own place." Some interpret this as meaning Judas went to a special place when he died, and he is now awaiting the time when he will be brought back as the Antichrist. Acts 1:25 is then correlated with Revelation 17:8, and that special place is usually identified as "the abyss" or the bottomless pit. Revelation 17:8 says, "The beast that you saw was, and is not, and is about to come up out of the abyss and go to destruction."

While it is certainly possible that the Antichrist will be Nero, Judas Iscariot, or some other nefarious individual from the past brought back to life, the Bible never clearly identifies any person from the past as potentially being the Antichrist. To explain the language in Revelation 13 and 17, it is not necessary to resort to a *past* individual who will be resurrected in the future. Rather, it seems better to view the Antichrist as a *future* individual who will die, then come back to life.

What other names and titles will he have?

Without any doubt, the title that most Christians use in reference to the coming end-time world ruler is *Antichrist*. That is the same title that even non-Christians are most familiar with today. But that is not the only term the Bible uses to speak about him.

It shouldn't surprise us that other names and titles are attributed to him as well. Just as the Lord Jesus Christ is known by different names and titles throughout Scripture, the one who will come to imitate and oppose Christ is also known by various designations. A.W. Pink said,

> It is only as we make a careful study of the various and numerous names and titles of the Lord Jesus Christ, that we are in a position to appreciate His infinite excellencies and the manifold relationships which He sustains. From an opposite standpoint the same is equally true of the Antichrist. As we pay careful attention to the different names and titles which are given to him, we then discover what a marvelously complete delineation the Holy Spirit has furnished us with of the person, character, and career of this monster of wickedness.[26]

Also, Satan, the one who will indwell and inspire the Antichrist, has many different names and titles in Scripture: devil, Lucifer, the dragon, the serpent, a roaring lion, an angel of light, the prince of the power of the air, the god of this age, the prince of this world, the evil one, and the tempter. It shouldn't surprise us that Antichrist has many aliases as well. Here are the top ten aliases for the coming Antichrist—aliases that help us to paint a composite portrait of the various aspects of his career and character.[27]

Titles of the Antichrist

1. The little horn

> While I was contemplating the horns, behold, another horn, a little one, came up among them, and three of the

first horns were pulled out by the roots before it; and behold, this horn possessed eyes like the eyes of a man and a mouth uttering great boasts (Daniel 7:8).

2. A king, insolent and skilled in intrigue

In the latter period of their rule, when the transgressors have run their course, a king will arise, insolent and skilled in intrigue. His power will be mighty, but not by his own power, and he will destroy to an extraordinary degree and prosper and perform his will; he will destroy mighty men and the holy people. And through his shrewdness he will cause deceit to succeed by his influence; and he will magnify himself in his heart, and he will destroy many while they are at ease. He will even oppose the Prince of princes, but he will be broken without human agency (Daniel 8:23-25).

3. The prince who is to come

After the sixty-two weeks the Messiah will be cut off and have nothing, and the people of the prince who is to come will destroy the city and the sanctuary. And its end will come with a flood; even to the end there will be war; desolations are determined (Daniel 9:26).

4. The one who makes desolate

He will make a firm covenant with the many for one week, but in the middle of the week he will put a stop to sacrifice and grain offering; and on the wing of abominations will come one who makes desolate, even until a complete destruction, one that is decreed, is poured out on the one who makes desolate (Daniel 9:27).

5. The king who does as he pleases

The king will do as he pleases, and he will exalt and magnify himself above every god and will speak monstrous
things against the God of gods; and he will prosper until
the indignation is finished, for that which is decreed will
be done. He will show no regard for the gods of his fathers
or for the desire of women, nor will he show regard for
any other god; for he will magnify himself above them all.
But instead he will honor a god of fortresses, a god whom
his fathers did not know; he will honor him with gold, silver, costly stones and treasures. He will take action against
the strongest of fortresses with the help of a foreign god;
he will give great honor to those who acknowledge him
and will cause them to rule over the many, and will parcel out land for a price.

At the end time the king of the South will collide with
him, and the king of the North will storm against him
with chariots, with horsemen and with many ships; and
he will enter countries, overflow them and pass through.
He will also enter the Beautiful Land, and many countries will fall; but these will be rescued out of his hand:
Edom, Moab and the foremost of the sons of Ammon.
Then he will stretch out his hand against other countries,
and the land of Egypt will not escape. But he will gain
control over the hidden treasures of gold and silver and
over all the precious things of Egypt; and Libyans and
Ethiopians will follow at his heels. But rumors from the
East and from the North will disturb him, and he will go
forth with great wrath to destroy and annihilate many.
He will pitch the tents of his royal pavilion between the
seas and the beautiful Holy Mountain; yet he will come
to his end, and no one will help him (Daniel 11:36-45).

6. A foolish shepherd

The LORD said to me, "Take again for yourself the equipment of a foolish shepherd. For behold, I am going to raise up a shepherd in the land who will not care for the perishing, seek the scattered, heal the broken, or sustain the one standing, but will devour the flesh of the fat sheep and tear off their hoofs. Woe to the worthless shepherd who leaves the flock! A sword will be on his arm and on his right eye! His arm will be totally withered and his right eye will be blind" (Zechariah 11:15-17).

7. The man of destruction

Let no one in any way deceive you, for it will not come unless the apostasy comes first, and the man of lawlessness is revealed, the son of destruction (2 Thessalonians 2:3).

8. The lawless one

That lawless one will be revealed whom the Lord will slay with the breath of His mouth and bring to an end by the appearance of His coming (2 Thessalonians 2:8).

9. The rider on the white horse

I looked, and behold, a white horse, and he who sat on it had a bow; and a crown was given to him, and he went out conquering and to conquer (Revelation 6:2).

10. The beast out of the sea

The dragon stood on the sand of the seashore. Then I saw a beast coming up out of the sea, having ten horns and

seven heads, and on his horns were ten diadems, and on
his heads were blasphemous names. And the beast which
I saw was like a leopard, and his feet were like those of
a bear, and his mouth like the mouth of a lion. And the
dragon gave him his power and his throne and great authority (Revelation 13:1-2).

Those titles leave little to the imagination. The final world
ruler will be the satanic superman.

Will he be a homosexual?

Upon reading that question you may find yourself wondering,
*Where did that question come from? Have other people asked about
that?* The answer is yes. I've been asked about this many times,
and the issue has arisen in many books about the end times. The
basis for this question comes from the wording found in the King
James Version and the New American Standard version of Daniel
11:37. They say that the coming Antichrist will not "regard…the
desire of women" (KJV) and "will show no regard…for the desire
of women" (NASB). Many students of Bible prophecy have taken
those statements to mean that the Antichrist will be a homosexual. They believe that as one who is totally controlled by Satan,
the Antichrist will live in complete disobedience to God in every
area of life, including his sexual orientation. The Antichrist is
viewed as sexually polluted, perverted, and profane.

While it's possible to interpret Daniel 11:37 in that way, notice the verse only explicitly says that the Antichrist will not have
a natural desire for women—not that he will have sexual desire
for men.

The phrase "desire of women" in Daniel 11:37 has been understood in various ways. First, some view it as a reference to

the Messiah. That's because it was the natural desire of all Jewish women in ancient Israel to be the mother of the Messiah who was promised in Genesis 3:15. Haggai 2:7, which refers to the Messiah as the "desire of all nations" (KJV), is often used to support this view. If one takes this viewpoint, it means that the Antichrist will reject all religion and will especially oppose the messianic hope.

Others take the Antichrist's rejection of the desire of women to refer to his lack of any of the graces of womanhood, such as kindness, love, and mercy. While that view is also possible, it seems best, in the context of this passage, to understand his lack of regard for the desire of women to indicate that the Antichrist will be so intoxicated with his love for power that it will totally consume all of his passion. His god is the god of military might and power. Daniel 11:38-39 helps to explain verse 37:

> Instead he will honor a god of fortresses, a god whom his fathers did not know; he will honor him with gold, silver, costly stones and treasures. He will take action against the strongest of fortresses with the help of a foreign god; he will give great honor to those who acknowledge him and will cause them to rule over the many, and will parcel out land for a price.

Whatever view one takes of the enigmatic phrase "the desire of women," I don't believe Daniel 11:37 should be used to suggest that the Antichrist will be a homosexual. Rather, he will be so enraptured with the god of military might, conquest, and political power that this obsession will eclipse any desire he would otherwise have for women.

What is the nationality of the Antichrist?

As you can imagine, there has been much speculation about the nationality or national origin of the Antichrist. People are naturally curious about where he will come from. I believe he will rise from a confederation of nations that in some way corresponds to the old Roman Empire. There are two major points in favor of this conclusion.

First, in both Daniel and the book of Revelation, the Antichrist is always associated with the final form of the Roman Empire. For us to understand this connection we need to go back about 2500 years ago to the time of the Jewish prophet Daniel, who was given a panoramic revelation by God that provided an overview of world history from Daniel's day all the way up to the second coming of Jesus Christ on planet Earth. Daniel's timeless prophecy is as relevant today as the day it was written. There are events taking place today that strikingly foreshadow his ancient message.

Daniel wrote most of his great prophecy in the middle of the sixth century BC, near the end of the 70-year Jewish exile in Babylon. God knew that during this time of discipline, His people would have all kinds of questions about what the future held. They were no doubt asking questions like, Is God finished with us? Will God be faithful to His covenant with Abraham to give us the land of Israel forever? Will the everlasting kingdom promised to David ever be realized? Will Messiah ever come to rule and reign over the earth?

In Daniel chapters 2 and 7, God encouraged His people and answered their questions by giving them a sweeping glimpse of the course of world history. God wanted them to know that His promises were sure and that He would keep His Word—that the promised kingdom would eventually come to Israel. However, God also wanted His people to know that the kingdom would not come immediately. Before the King and His kingdom would come, four great world empires would rule over Israel in succession. With the benefit of 20/20 hindsight we now know that these four empires were Babylon, Medo-Persia, Greece, and Rome. In Daniel 2 these four empires are pictured as parts of a great metallic statue that king Nebuchadnezzar saw in a dream. Each part was made from a different metal:

The Metallic Statue in Daniel 2

Head of gold	Babylon
Arms and chest of silver	Medo-Persia
Stomach and thighs of bronze	Greece
Legs of iron	Rome

Up to this point, almost everyone is in general agreement about the meaning of Nebuchadnezzar's dream in Daniel 2. The disagreement begins with regard to the final form of the Roman Empire, which is pictured by the feet and ten toes of iron and baked clay. According to Daniel 2:42-44, the ten toes of the statue represent ten kings who will rule simultaneously just before the return of Jesus back to earth to establish His kingdom.

In Daniel 7, these same world empires are pictured again, but this time as four wild beasts that Daniel saw rising up out of the Mediterranean Sea.

The Four Beasts in Daniel 7

Winged lion	Babylon
Bloodthirsty bear	Medo-Persia
Leopard with four heads and two wings	Greece
Terrible beast	Rome

Just as in Daniel 2, the number ten appears in connection with the final empire described in the vision. In Daniel 2, there were ten toes on the feet of the statue. In Daniel 7, the terrifying beast that symbolizes the final form of the Roman Empire has ten horns (Daniel 7:7). The beast corresponds to the statue's legs of iron, and the ten horns correspond to the statue's ten toes. So, the final phase of the Roman Empire is depicted by ten horns, which are identified as ten kings (Daniel 7:24). Many have interpreted these ten toes and ten horns as nations or regions into which the world will be divided during the end times. But Daniel 2:44 and 7:24 clearly identify them as kings or individuals who will form some kind of ruling committee. These ten leaders may represent various nations or groups of nations, but the Bible never says so specifically. What we are told is that ten leaders will come together to form a reunited Roman Empire. These same ten end-time leaders are mentioned by the apostle John in Revelation 17:12-13, where they are described as "ten horns."

Some who read Daniel 2 and 7 believe that the ten toes and ten horns are already a part of past history—that they were part of the historical Roman Empire that was destroyed in AD 476. Yet we know from history that the Roman Empire never existed in a ten-king form as required by both Daniel 2 and 7. Moreover, according to Daniel 2 and 7, the final form of the Roman

Empire will experience complete, sudden destruction. Note that the image in Daniel 2 will suddenly be smashed to pieces, and then the dust will be blown away. But history documents for us that the Roman Empire deteriorated gradually until the western part of the empire fell in AD 476 and the eastern part was cut off in AD 1453. A more gradual process could hardly be imagined. The fact the Roman Empire declined slowly over a long period of time tells us that the sudden destruction prophesied in Daniel 2 has yet to be fulfilled.

The principal reason for believing that the ancient Roman Empire will one day be revived is the simple fact that prophecy requires it to happen. The various Bible prophecies dealing with the final phase of this empire have not been literally fulfilled in the same way as the prophecies about the preceding world empires. To those who believe the Bible, the prophecies of the future are just as authentic as the prophecies already fulfilled in history. If all the prophecies of Daniel 2 and 7 have known literal fulfillment except for those prophecies dealing with the final form of the Roman Empire, we must conclude that there is yet to come a revived Roman Empire that will experience a swift and total destruction.

This revived Roman Empire, according to Daniel, will emerge prior to the return of Christ, who will then set up His kingdom and reign over the earth. This final manifestation of the Roman Empire will take the form of a coalition or confederation of ten world leaders (symbolized by the ten toes in Daniel 2 and the ten horns in Daniel 7) whose nations will encompass the same basic geographical territory as the original or historical Roman Empire. We are told that the little horn of Daniel 7:8, who is the coming Antichrist, will rise up among these ten kings, which connects the Antichrist to this reunited Roman Empire. Therefore, we can see that the Bible pictures the Antichrist as coming from a group of nations that correspond in some way to the old Roman Empire.

A second main point in favor of the Roman origin of the Antichrist also comes from the book of Daniel. As far as I am aware, the only passage in Scripture that conclusively tells us about the Antichrist's nationality is Daniel 9:26, which states that Antichrist ("the prince who is to come") will be of the same nationality as the people who destroyed the second Jewish Temple in AD 70. Daniel 9:26 tells us, "The people of the prince who is to come [the coming Antichrist] will destroy the city and the sanctuary." Of course, we know from history that the Romans destroyed the Temple in Jerusalem. Therefore, we know that the Antichrist will be of Roman origin. This doesn't mean necessarily that he will be Italian, but simply that he will rise from somewhere within the reunited Roman Empire. This limits his place of origin to Europe, the Middle East, or north Africa. Most people have taken this to mean that he will come out of one of the nations of Europe that formed the nucleus of the old Roman Empire, possibly even Rome itself. This formed the core of the Roman Empire that existed in the apostle John's day when he prophesied Antichrist's coming from a future form of the Roman Empire. Interestingly, the classic movie *The Omen* picked up on this idea and opened with the birth of the Antichrist in a dimly lit hospital in Rome. A chilling poem from this same movie reinforces the belief that the coming Antichrist will arise from a reborn Holy Roman Empire.

As we look at the global scene today, we see that large numbers of Jewish people have returned to Zion (Israel), and the ancient Roman Empire is rising before our eyes in the form of the European Community. Different nations that were once part of what comprised the ancient Roman Empire are coming back together like the feet and toes of iron and clay in Daniel 2. These nations are coming together in a diverse mixture of strong and weak countries that don't adhere very well to one another (just as iron and clay don't mix well), which is causing internal problems. The rise of Antichrist from this amalgamation may not be far behind!

Will he be a Muslim, possibly even the Islamic Mahdi?

There are a growing number of prophecy teachers and authors who claim that the coming Antichrist or world ruler will be a Muslim, or that he will be the manifestation of the Islamic messiah (Mahdi). Given the meteoric rise of Islam on the international scene, it is not surprising that this view is becoming more popular. Those who hold this view generally reject the idea of a reunited Roman Empire centered in Europe as the dominant force in the end times. For them, the world will be dominated by a Muslim caliphate and ruled over by the Islamic messiah.

The reasoning behind this view is as follows: First, proponents often point to the basic fact that Islam is the fastest-growing religion in the world—even in the United States, Canada, and Europe. In a very short time, Islam will pass Christianity as the world's largest religion. Thus they argue that it simply makes sense that the world's final military, political, and spiritual leader will come from this majority religion. My response to this point is that we must be careful not to interpret prophecy in light of current events, but rather, view current events through the lens of Scripture. Looking at biblical prophecy through the headlines is often called "newspaper exegesis" and can lead to unwarranted conclusions and sensationalism.

Second, adherents of this view sometimes note that the vast majority of the nations that the Bible lists as key end-time players are currently Islamic nations, including Syria, Jordan, Egypt, Sudan, Libya, Lebanon, Turkey, and Iran. Because these are among the key end-time nations, proponents argue that it makes most sense if the coming world ruler is a Muslim from one of these nations. They also usually hold that Gog (in Ezekiel 38–39), the leader of an end-time invasion against Israel, is the same person as the Antichrist (we will address that issue later). While it is true that the staging ground for the end times is the nation of Israel, we have to keep in mind the involvement of the final form of the Roman Empire as indicated by Daniel 2 and 7. Also, Ezekiel 38 refers to "Rosh," which many believe is modern-day Russia. What's more, Revelation 16:12 also identifies a great military confederation that will come from east of the Euphrates River. This confederation, led by "the kings from the east," will pour into the Middle East in the end times. So the claim that "all the nations" mentioned in end-time prophecy are Islamic is an overstatement. Other key nations and joint forces will have major roles as well.

Third, proponents of this view point to the many similarities between the Muslim Mahdi or messiah and the biblical Antichrist. For example, both will be world rulers, both will be spiritual world leaders, both will make seven-year treaties, and both will ride on a white horse.[28] These similarities are cited as proof that these two end-time figures are one and the same. But consider this: Isn't it possible that the reason for the similarities is that Muhammed obtained much of his information about the last days from the Bible stories he heard from Jews and Christians?

Fourth, the Bible says that the Antichrist will bring terrible persecution upon the Jewish people. Those who hold to the Islamic Antichrist position note that the Mahdi will launch a targeted campaign against Jews and Christians, will attack Israel, and will establish the seat of his authority on the Temple Mount, just as the Bible predicts in 2 Thessalonians 2:4. They also point out that the Temple Mount is currently under Muslim control. They believe all those points are consistent with the possibility the Antichrist will be a Muslim. However, it seems very unlikely that an Islamic Mahdi would sit in a rebuilt Jewish Temple to declare himself God. Any Muslim "worth his salt" would *destroy* the Jewish Temple—not sit in it.

Fifth, some proponents highlight the fact that the Antichrist will use beheading as a form of execution against those who reject his rule (Revelation 20:4). They hasten to point out that this is a favorite means of execution among followers of Islam. While this is true, beheading was also the chief method of execution in the French Revolution, and whatever his background, the Antichrist could revive this form of execution because it's simple, swift, and would instill great fear in those who are thinking about rejecting his rule.

Sixth, Daniel 7:25 says of the coming Antichrist that "he will speak out against the Most High and wear down the saints of the Highest One, and he will intend to make alterations in times and in law; and they will be given into his hand for a time, times, and half a time." Joel Richardson views this as a key clue that the Antichrist will be the Muslim Mahdi. He says,

> This is actually quite a big hint into the person of the Antichrist. For by his actions, we see a hint of his origin. It is said that he will desire to change two things; times and laws. Now we have already seen that the Mahdi will change the law by instituting the Islamic Shariah law all over the earth, but we have not seen any evidence in Islamic apocalyptic literature of him changing the "times." The simple question however is, who else other than a

Muslim would desire to change the "times and laws?"…
Islam however, does have both its own laws and its own
calendar, both of which it would desire to impose onto
the entire world. The Islamic calendar is based on the career of Muhammad.[29]

It is obviously true that the Muslims have a calendar different
from the Western world, and it is true that if they ever could gain
control of the world, they would enforce the observance of their
calendar. However, the Antichrist is going to change the calendar regardless of who he is or what his religious background may
be because the calendar followed by most of the world counts
time from the birth of Jesus. The Antichrist's changing of times
and laws will be his attempt to remove any vestige of Christianity from society. It's not necessary for the Antichrist to be the Islamic Mahdi to fulfill this prophecy.[30]

The only passage of Scripture I know of that gives insight into
the religious background of the Antichrist is found in Daniel
11:36-39. Describing the final world ruler as "the king [who] will
do as he pleases," Daniel said,

> He will exalt and magnify himself above every god…He
> will show no regard for the gods of his fathers or for the
> desire of women, nor will he show regard for any other
> god; for he will magnify himself above them all. But in-
> stead he will honor a god of fortresses, a god whom his
> fathers did not know; he will honor him with gold, silver,
> costly stones and treasures. He will take action against
> the strongest of fortresses with the help of a foreign god.

While I would agree that there are some interesting parallels
between the biblical Antichrist and the Islamic Mahdi, for me,
this passage precludes the Islamic Antichrist view. Daniel said

the Antichrist will exalt himself above *every* god and will honor a god that his fathers did not know. The Antichrist could be someone who was a Muslim at some point in his life, but if that were the case, for him to "honor a god that his fathers did not know" would mean he would have to reject Allah and turn to another god—the god of fortresses or military might, and ultimately himself. So, even if he were a Muslim at some point in his life, which is possible, this passage makes it clear that when he comes to power he will have turned his back on all religion and established himself as god.

Second Thessalonians 2:4 states that the Antichrist will take his seat in the Temple of God, which is a reference to a rebuilt or third Jewish Temple in Jerusalem, and will declare that he is god. No practicing Muslim could ever do this. Certainly the Islamic Mahdi could never do this. To do so would violate the central tenet of Islam that there is one God, who is Allah. If the Antichrist pronounced himself god, he would no longer be a follower of Islam. Joel Richardson, who supports the Muslim Antichrist view, acknowledges this problem yet responds in this way:

> We need to understand that the Antichrist will not demand worship until well after the fact that he has been universally acknowledged and accepted by the Islamic world as the Mahdi. The Imams, mullahs, sheiks, and the Ayatollahs, all of the world Islamic leadership, will have given their allegiance to the Mahdi. To deny him after this point would be the ultimate shame for Islam. It would come at a time when Islam will universally be experiencing its greatest rush of vindication and fulfillment. In the midst of all this incredible elation, to suddenly declare and acknowledge that an absolute evil charlatan had deceived the entire Islamic world would

be unthinkable. Once the deception has taken place, it
will be impossible to undo. The hook will have been set.[31]

This answer overlooks the fact that the Antichrist's declaration
of himself as god will be the ultimate act of brazen blasphemy. No
self-respecting Muslim could ever accept such a scenario. To believe that Islamic leaders would still follow someone who claimed
to be the Islamic Mahdi and then later declared himself to be God
is naïve. If the modern rise of radical Islam teaches us anything,
it's that their leaders are ardent zealots unwilling to compromise
on lesser points of religious practice, let alone the major tenet of
their faith.

For these reasons, I don't hold to the Islamic Antichrist view.
I believe the Bible teaches that he will be a God-hating, Christ-
rejecting megalomaniac who will despise every religion and every
god other than himself and his ultimate master, Satan.

Could an American president be
the Antichrist?

As was noted in chapter 1, almost every American president
since John F. Kennedy has been alleged to be the Antichrist—
usually by someone of the opposing political party. There are
some people who speculate that because the U.S. president is generally considered the most powerful individual on earth, perhaps
one of them will be the Antichrist. They reason that according
to Scripture, the Antichrist will rise from a reunited Roman Empire. Because America was formed out of the nations of Europe,
derived its language and laws from Rome, and is the most powerful nation in the world, they wonder if, by extension, the Antichrist could come from the United States.

But that seems highly unlikely to me. It seems best to hold

that the Antichrist will come out of a future form of the Roman Empire that existed in John's day when he prophesied about the Antichrist's coming. Extending the boundaries of the Roman Empire to include America just because the nation was founded by Europeans is a stretch. But regardless of where he comes from, one thing is certain: He is coming. And he will do exactly what the Bible predicts he will do.

Is the Antichrist the same person as "Gog" in Ezekiel 38?

Ezekiel 38–39 is one of the key Old Testament prophecies of the end times. It predicts a massive invasion of Israel by a confederation of surrounding nations. The alliance of nations is listed in Ezekiel 38:1-6:

> The word of the LORD came to me saying, "Son of man, set your face toward Gog of the land of Magog, the prince of Rosh, Meshech and Tubal, and prophesy against him and say, 'Thus says the Lord GOD, "Behold, I am against you, O Gog, prince of Rosh, Meshech and Tubal. I will turn you about and put hooks into your jaws, and I will bring you out, and all your army, horses and horsemen, all of them splendidly attired, a great company with buckler and shield, all of them wielding swords; Persia, Ethiopia and Put with them, all of them with shield and helmet; Gomer with all its troops; Beth-togarmah from the remote parts of the north with all its troops—many peoples with you."'"

What are the locations of the ancient places Ezekiel listed back in 570 BC? A look at the map reveals the modern nations that occupy those ancient lands. They are Russia (Rosh), the nations of central Asia (Magog), Turkey (Meshech, Tubal, Gomer, Togar-mah), Iran (Persia), Sudan (Cush), and Libya (Put). All of these nations are Islamic today except Russia.

Sometime during the first half of the Tribulation, when Israel is at peace and living securely under her treaty with the Antichrist, Russia and this host of Islamic allies will mount an all-out attack of the land of Israel. The leader of this invasion is called "Gog" in Ezekiel 38:2. The name Gog appears in the Old Testament only one time outside Ezekiel 38–39—we find it in 1 Chronicles 5:4, where Gog is listed as one of the descendants of Reuben. The Gog in that passage has no relation to the one mentioned in Ezekiel.

The name "Gog" appears eleven times in Ezekiel 38–39, more than any other name in the chapter. It's clear from reading the references to Gog that he is a person who leads the aforementioned invasion against Israel. Therefore, we know that Gog is the most important person in this coalition. Gog is clearly the leading actor in this great drama during the end times. His name means "high, supreme, a height or a high mountain." The way his name is used in Ezekiel reveals that Gog is a person who comes from the ancient land of Magog, or the southern part of the former Soviet Union. Gog is probably not a person's name but a symbolic kingly title like Pharaoh, Caesar, czar, or president. The term "prince" is also used in reference to Gog in Ezekiel 38–39.

There's a growing view that Gog is simply another title for the Antichrist, and that the invasion in Ezekiel 38 is the battle of Armageddon. Joel Richardson is among those who support equating Antichrist with Gog:

> I personally reject the idea that Gog is anyone other than
> Antichrist…Simply stated, Antichrist is Satan's puppet that
> he will use to attack Jerusalem. And at least in the Book of

Revelation, Gog is also Satan's puppet that will serve the very same purpose. In terms of both role and function, Antichrist and the Gog of Revelation are essentially the same...Those who view Ezekiel's Gog as a competitor to the Antichrist find themselves taking a very inconsistent position...Gog and the Antichrist are one and the same.[32]

There are others, however, who believe this identification is erroneous. We must keep in mind that Gog leads a Russian-Islamic invasion force, not the reunited Roman Empire prophesied about Antichrist in Daniel 7 and in Revelation 13 and 17. Gog is called "the king of the North" in Daniel 11:40, and his invasion of Israel will pose a direct challenge to the Antichrist's treaty with Israel. That would make it impossible for Gog to be the Antichrist. Rather, Gog is a ruler over Russia who will lead her and her allies to their doom in Israel during the Tribulation period.

Gog	Antichrist
King of the North	King of the West
Attacks Israel	Makes a treaty with Israel (later breaks it)

Also, it's important to remember that the invasion described in Ezekiel 38, which is led by Gog, is not the same as the battle of Armageddon, which is led by the Antichrist. The campaign of Armageddon, headed up by the Antichrist, will takes place at the end of the Tribulation, whereas the invasion in Ezekiel 38 will take place during the first half of the Tribulation when Israel is "living securely" and "at rest" (Ezekiel 38:8,11,14). Here is a chart that shows seven of the key differences between these two last-days' battles.

Gog and Magog (Ezekiel 38–39)	Armageddon (Revelation 19)
Invasion is led by Gog	Invasion is led by Antichrist
Israel is at peace at the time of the invasion	There is no mention of peace in Israel
Armies gather to plunder Israel	Armies gather to fight against Christ
Occurs at the middle of the Tribulation	Occurs at the end of the Tribulation
Specific nations (Russia and her Islamic allies)	All nations invade Israel
Armies are destroyed by the supernatural judgment of God, including the members of the coalition turning on each other	Armies are destroyed by the second coming of Christ
Occurs so that all the nations will know that He is God	Occurs to destroy the nations

While I believe that Gog and the Antichrist are two different end-time players, I also believe that they are related to one another in a very important way. To understand this connection we must realize that Gog's strike force will be annihilated by God. When Gog and his armies pour into Israel, it will look like the biggest mismatch in military history. It will look like Israel is finished. But God will intervene in what we might call not the Six-Day War, but the One-Day War (or One-Hour War). Ezekiel 38:18-23 graphically describes the cataclysmic destruction of Gog and his army by the supernatural power of God:

"It will come about on that day, when Gog comes against the land of Israel," declares the Lord GOD, "that My fury will mount up in My anger. In My zeal and in My blazing wrath I declare that on that day there will surely be a great earthquake in the land of Israel. The fish of the sea, the birds of the heavens, the beasts of the field, all the creeping things that creep on the earth, and all the men who are on the face of the earth will shake at My presence; the mountains also will be thrown down, the steep pathways will collapse and every wall will fall to the ground. I will call for a sword against him on all My mountains," declares the Lord GOD. "Every man's sword will be against his brother. With pestilence and with blood I will enter into judgment with him; and I will rain on him and on his troops, and on the many peoples who are with him, a torrential rain, with hailstones, fire and brimstone. I will magnify Myself, sanctify Myself, and make Myself known in the sight of many nations; and they will know that I am the LORD."

Here's the connection I see between this destruction of Gog and the rise of Antichrist: When Gog and his massive coalition are destroyed during the first half of the Tribulation, a profound power vacuum will open up, and the Antichrist will move quickly to fill it. The elimination of this Russian-Islamic alliance and all their troops will pave the way for the Antichrist to posture himself to take over the world at the midpoint of the Tribulation and declare himself to be God. I've often wondered if the Antichrist might even take credit for the destruction of Gog's army by claiming he has a secret weapon of mass destruction that he used to annihilate them. He could use this propaganda to intimidate the rest of the world into following him in what will become a global reign of terror.

Is the mark of the beast (666) past or future?

One of the most fascinating topics related to the coming Antichrist is the mysterious mark of the beast. All kinds of questions swirl around the meaning and application of this mark. And one of the questions being asked a lot these days is this: Were the prophecies about the mark of the beast fulfilled in the past, or is this mark something that still lies in the future?

Those scholars who hold to a preterist view of the book of Revelation—that is, they say most or all of the events described in Revelation have already taken place—maintain that the mark of the beast was used during the reign of the Roman ruler Nero (AD 54–68).[33] Preterists say that most or all the prophecies in Revelation, as well as the rest of the New Testament, were fulfilled during the Jewish War (AD 66–70) and the destruction of Jerusalem in AD 70. For them, the Antichrist is not a "future foe; he is a relic of history."[34] Antichrist, in their view, has already appeared on the scene and been defeated by Christ. To the preterists, Nero was the beast.

Preterists argue that the Greek form of Nero's name, *Neron Caesar,* written in Hebrew characters, adds up to the number 666. They further claim that some ancient Greek manuscripts contain the variant number 616 instead of 666 and that the Latin form of Nero's name, *Nero Caesar,* is equivalent to the number 616.[35] Proponents of the preterist view also say Nero's persecution of Christians lasted about 42 months or 1260 days, which corresponds to the length of time mentioned in Revelation 13:5.[36]

However, there are serious difficulties with identifying Nero as the beast who comes "up out of the sea" (Revelation 13:1). First, the book of Revelation was written in AD 95, almost 30 years after the reign of Nero was already over. Therefore, Revelation 13:1 can't be a prophecy about him.[37] In fact, the date of the writing of Revelation is the most stubborn problem for the entire preterist viewpoint. The traditional, dominant view of the church—from the second century all the way up through today—is that Revelation was written near the end of Domitian's reign. All of the luminaries in the early church who addressed this issue held to the AD 95 date. This eliminates the preterist view as a viable alternative, including its belief that Nero was the beast of Revelation 13:1.

Second, in claiming that Nero was the beast, preterists Gary DeMar and Kenneth Gentry interpret the 42 months of the beast's worldwide reign as a literal event. But at the same time, DeMar and Gentry assign a symbolic interpretation to almost all the other numbers in Revelation. Why do they take the 42 months of Antichrist's rule literally yet take the other numbers symbolically? There is no justification in the Bible text for their inconsistent approach to the numbers in Revelation.

Third, and most importantly, Nero never fulfilled a number of other clear prophetic statements in Revelation 13. Here are just a few examples:

1. The beast will be worshiped by the *entire* world: "All who dwell on the earth will worship him, everyone whose name has not been written from the foundation of the world in the book of life of the Lamb who has been slain" (Revelation 13:8). All classes of humanity will be forced to take sides: "the small and the great, and the rich and the poor, and the free men and the slaves" (Revelation 13:16). Robert Thomas, a noted New Testament scholar, notes that this language "extends to all

people of every civic rank…all classes ranked according to wealth…covers every cultural category…The three expressions are a formula for universality."[38]

2. He will force people to take his mark on their right hand or forehead if they want to engage in any commercial transactions.

3. The false prophet will erect an image of the beast and force all the world to worship the beast.

4. The beast will be slain and come back to life.

5. The beast in Revelation 13:1-10 will have an associate, the false prophet, who will call down fire from heaven and give breath to the image (13:11-18).

Clearly, none of those prophecies were fulfilled during Nero's reign. Neither Nero, nor any other Roman emperor, ever marked the whole world with the mark of the beast, or 666. Nero had no assistant or propaganda minister who fits the description of the false prophet as given in Revelation 13.[39] Those prophecies remain unfulfilled and will not come about until the Antichrist arises during the end times.

Fourth, in order for Nero's name to equal the number 666, you have to use the precise title *Neron Caesar.* No other form of his name will work. Moreover, there is an abbreviated form of the name *Domitian* (the Roman Caesar from AD 81–96) that also equals 666.[40] Revelation 13:17 says specifically that the number equals "the name of the beast or the number of his name." *Neron Caesar* was not Nero's name. The word *Caesar* is a title, not part of his name. To do that is like adding the word *president* before a person's name and including that as part of his name. That goes beyond what the text of Revelation 13:17 says about the number 666.

Fifth, if the connection between 666 and Nero is so obvious, as preterists claim, why did it take almost 1800 years after Nero's death for anyone to realize it?[41] All the early church fathers who wrote after the time of Nero adopted a futurist view of the beast out of the sea and the number 666.[42] The first people who suggested a connection between Nero and 666 were four German scholars in the 1830s.[43]

Revelation 13:17-18 clearly says that the number 666 will be the mark proposed for the right hand or forehead. No one in history, including Nero, has ever proposed such a number or mark during times that approach the scenario that will unfold during the Tribulation. So past guesses as to the Antichrist's identity can be nullified on this basis. Robert Thomas provides wise guidance in this area:

> The better part of wisdom is to be content that the identification is not yet available, but will be when the future false Christ ascends to his throne. The person to whom 666 applies must have been future to John's time, because John clearly meant the number to be recognizable to someone. If it was not discernible to his generation and those immediately following him—and it was not—the generation to whom it will be discernible must have lain (and still lies) in the future. Past generations have provided many illustrations of this future personage, but all past candidates have proven inadequate as fulfillments.[44]

Nero did not fulfill—nor has any other past person fulfilled—the detailed prophecies given in Revelation 13:1-10. The only conclusion we can reach, then, is that the mark of the beast is still future.

What is the mark of the beast?

The number 666, the so-called mark of the beast, may be one of the most intriguing issues in all of Bible prophecy. There has probably been more speculation, sensationalism, and silliness prompted by this issue than any other one I can think of in Bible prophecy. And as time has moved forward, the true meaning of the mark seems to have almost gotten lost. The number has been increasingly trivialized as people have worked overtime to associate it with almost anything that has no association with Bible prophecy. A few years ago I came across a list of some of the absurd applications:

Route 666	The way of the beast
00666	The zip code of the beast
Phillips 666	The gasoline of the beast
LXVI	The Roman numeral of the beast
666k	The retirement plan of the beast
999	The Australian number of the beast
IAM666	The license plate of the beast
666i	BMW of the beast

What's tragic about all this trivialization is that the number 666 is a serious issue. After all, it's connected with the Antichrist—a future world ruler who will bring great evil and destruction upon the earth.

Revelation 13:16-18 is the biblical key that opens the door to the meaning of 666—the mark of the beast—and the coming one-world economy with its accompanying cashless society. This passage is the biblical entry point for any discussion about the number 666:

> He causes all, the small and the great, and the rich and the poor, and the free men and the slaves, to be given a mark on their right hand or on their forehead, and he provides that no one will be able to buy or to sell, except the one who has the mark, either the name of the beast or the number of his name. Here is wisdom. Let him who has understanding calculate the number of the beast, for the number is that of a man; and his number is six hundred and sixty-six.

Having determined that this mark of the beast is future, the next thing we need to do is define the nature of this mark. The Bible teaches that during the Tribulation the false prophet, who is the head of the Antichrist's religious propaganda machine, will head up the campaign of the mark of the beast (Revelation 13:11-18). Revelation 13:15 makes it clear that the key issue underlying the mark of the beast is "worship [of] the image of the beast." The mark of the beast is simply a vehicle to force people to declare their allegiance—to either the Antichrist or Jesus Christ. Everyone will be polarized into two camps, for it will be impossible to take a neutral stance. Scripture says those who refuse to receive the mark will be killed (Revelation 20:4).

All classes of humanity will be forced to take sides: "the small and the great, and the rich and the poor, and the free men and the slaves" (Revelation 13:16). Scripture is very specific: The false prophet will require a mark of loyalty and devotion to the beast, and it will be "on their right hand"—not the left—or it will be "on their forehead" (Revelation 13:16).

But what is this mark?

We find the word "mark" sprinkled throughout the Bible. For example, it is used many times in Leviticus in reference to a mark that renders the bearer ceremonially unclean, such as when someone has leprosy. Clearly, in those cases, the "mark" is something external and visible.

Interestingly, Ezekiel 9:4 uses "mark" in a way that is similar to how it's used in Revelation: "The LORD said to him, 'Go through the midst of the city, even through the midst of Jerusalem, and put *a mark on the foreheads* of the men who sigh and groan over all the abominations which are being committed in its midst.'" Here the mark was one of preservation—similar to the way the lamb's blood on the doorposts of Israelite homes in Egypt spared their firstborn from the death angel (Exodus 12:7-13). In Ezekiel, the mark is placed visibly on the foreheads of certain individuals, which anticipates the apostle John's use of the term in Revelation.

Eight out of the nine uses of the word translated "mark" or "sign" in the Greek New Testament appear in Revelation, and all refer to the mark of the beast (Revelation 13:16; 13:17; 14:9; 14:11; 16:2; 19:20; 20:4). The word "mark" in Greek (*charagma*) means "a mark or stamp engraved, etched, branded, cut, imprinted."[45] Robert Thomas explains how the word was used in ancient times:

> The mark must be some sort of branding similar to that given soldiers, slaves, and temple devotees in John's day. In Asia Minor, devotees of pagan religions delighted in the display of such a tattoo as an emblem of ownership by a certain god. In Egypt, Ptolemy Philopator I branded Jews, who submitted to registration, with an ivy leaf in recognition of their Dionysian worship (cf. 3 *Macc.* 2:29). This meaning resembles the long-time practice of carrying signs to advertise religious loyalties (cf. Isa. 44:5) and follows the habit of branding slaves with the name or special mark of their owners (cf. Gal. 6:17). *Charagma* ("Mark") was a term for the images or names of emperors

on Roman coins, so it fittingly could apply to the beast's emblem put on people.[46]

Henry Morris also provides an excellent description of the nature of the mark:

> The nature of the mark is not described, but the basic principle has been established for years in various nations. The social security card, the draft registration card, the practice of stenciling an inked design on the back of the hand, and various other devices are all forerunners of this universal branding. The word itself ("mark") is the Greek *charagma*. It is used only in Revelation, to refer to the mark of the beast (eight times), plus one time to refer to idols "graven by art and man's device" (Acts 17:29). The mark is something like an etching or a tattoo which, once inscribed, cannot be removed, providing a permanent (possibly eternal) identification as a follower of the beast and the dragon.[47]

The issue for each person alive during the Tribulation will be this: Will I swear allegiance to the man who claims to be God? Will I give up ownership of my life to him by taking his mark, or will I bow the knee to the true God and lose my right to buy and sell and even face beheading (Revelation 20:4)? Taking the mark will ultimately be a spiritual decision; the economic benefits will be secondary to this momentous choice every person will face.

What's the significance of the number 666?

In the movie *The Omen*, Damien was born on June 6, at 6:00 (666) to symbolize his identification as the coming Antichrist. Almost everyone—even those who are biblically illiterate—has heard something about 666 or the mark of the beast. I remember all the furor over the date June 6, 2006 (6/6/06). I was interviewed by dozens of radio stations and appeared on Fox News to discuss the superstition surrounding that day. One radio station even went so far as to offer presents to the parents of any child born on that day.

As you can imagine, there are multiple explanations for what 666 means. I believe the best answer includes the use of a process called *gematria,* which refers to the numerical value of names. In gematria, a numerical value is attributed to each of the letters of the alphabet. If you want to find the numerical total of a word or name, you add together the numerical value of each individual letter in the word or name. Clearly, in Revelation 13, some kind of numerical value is connected to the beast's name, for we are told that the one with "wisdom" is to "calculate" or count the number.[48] To count the number of a name simply means to add up the numbers attached to all the letters that appear in the name.[49]

Hebrew, Latin, Greek, and English all have numerical values for each letter in the alphabet. For example, each letter in the 22-letter Hebrew alphabet is assigned a numerical value as follows: 1, 2, 3, 4, 5, 6, 7, 8, 9, 10, 20, 30, 40, 50, 60, 70, 80, 90, 100, 200, 300, and 400.

Revelation 13:16-18 provides five key clues that aid in the interpretation of the mark of the beast—clues that I believe support the idea that gematria is involved in some way. Read Revelation 13:17-18 and notice the progression of the phrases listed below:

1. "the name of the beast"
2. "the number of his name"
3. "the number of the beast"
4. "the number is that of a man"
5. "his number is six hundred and sixty-six"[50]

When these five clues are followed in their logical progression, we see that the number or mark of the beast is the number of a man who is the Antichrist or final world ruler. This number is the number of the Antichrist's own name.

As prophecy scholar Arnold Fruchtenbaum notes:

> In this passage whatever the personal name of the Antichrist will be, if his name is spelled out in Hebrew characters, the numerical value of his name will be 666. So this is the number that will be put on the worshipers of the Antichrist. Since a number of different calculations can equal 666, it is impossible to figure the name out in advance. But when he does appear, whatever his personal name will be, it will equal 666. Those who are wise (verse 18) at that time will be able to point him out.[51]

When the Antichrist begins to appear on the world scene at the beginning of the Tribulation, those who have an understanding of God's Word will be able to identify him by the number of his name. The numerical value of his name will be 666.

Many have grossly misused the gematria approach by applying it to the names of modern leaders to see if they could be the Antichrist. It has been applied to Henry Kissinger and Lyndon Johnson, and I have been told that both of their names equal the number 666. It has also been tried out on John F. Kennedy, Gorbachev, and Ronald Reagan. Supposedly Bill Gates III equals 666. And allegedly MS DOS 6.21 equals 666, as does Windows 95 and System 7.0.

I recently received a call from a man who emphatically told me that Philip Borbon Carlos, the son of Juan Carlos of Spain, is the Antichrist because each of his three names contains six letters, and he is a prominent European leader. Yet telephone directories are *full* of names that will add up to 666 when the individual letters are converted to their numerical value. That reveals the absurdity of attempting to "count the name" in our day. The instruction to "calculate the number of the beast" cannot be applied in our day, for that would be jumping the gun. Instead, it is to be applied by believers during the Tribulation. Speculating on the identity of the Antichrist is foolish and should be avoided. He will not be unveiled until the beginning of the Tribulation period, or "the day of the Lord" (2 Thessalonians 2:2-3). At that time people will be able to identify him because the number of his name will be 666.

Why 666?

Why did the Lord plan for the Antichrist's name to somehow equal 666? Many prophecy teachers have pointed out that the triple six refers to man's number, which is the number six, or one short of God's perfect number, which is seven. Remember, man was created on the sixth day. Prophecy scholar John Walvoord wrote,

> Though there may be more light cast on it at the time this prophecy is fulfilled, the passage itself declares that this number is "man's number." In the Book of Revelation, the number "7" is one of the most significant numbers, indicating perfection. Accordingly, there are seven seals, seven trumpets, seven bowls of the wrath of God, seven thunders, etc. This beast claims to be God, and if that were the case, he should be 777. This passage, in effect, says, No, you are only 666. You are short of deity even though you were originally created in the image and likeness of God. Most of the speculation on the meaning of this number is without profit or theological significance.[52]

M.R. DeHaan, the founder of Radio Bible Class, also held this position:

> Six is the number of man. Three is the number of divinity. Here is the interpretation. The beast will be a man who claims to be God. Three sixes imply that he is a false god and a deceiver, but he is nevertheless merely a man, regardless of his claims. Seven is the number of divine perfection, and 666 is one numeral short of seven. This man of sin will reach the highest peak of power and wisdom, but he will still be merely a man.[53]

I find it interesting that the number of the name *Jesus*, in Greek, is 888, and each of His eight names in the New Testament (Lord, Jesus, Christ, Lord Jesus, Jesus Christ, Christ Jesus, Lord Christ, and Lord Jesus Christ) all have numerical values that are multiples of eight.[54] I don't believe this is merely a coincidence. Jesus is complete perfection, while man, apart from God, is a complete, utter failure.

Adam, the first man, was created on the sixth day, while Jesus, the second man, was raised from the dead on Sunday, the "eighth day" of the week (the second first day of the week).[55] The use of the number 666 is God's way of demonstrating that the Antichrist, Satan's masterpiece, is nothing more than a fallen man who is completely under the control of the sovereign God of the ages.

What's the purpose of the mark?

When we read about the mark of the beast, one question that immediately comes to mind is this: Why will this mark be required? According to Scripture, the mark will serve two main purposes. First, as we have already noted, it will serve as a visible indicator of a person's devotion to Antichrist. Antichrist's mark, the numerical value of his name, will be etched or imprinted on the right hand or forehead of those who bow the knee to his iron fist. The mark of the beast will be a satanic counterfeit of the seal of God that is placed on the foreheads of the saints, which is the seal of the Holy Spirit (Revelation 7:3).[56] This is just another way Satan will mimic the work of God during the end times. The mark of the beast will serve as a kind of global pledge of allegiance, a visible sign that declares a person has bought into the Antichrist's vision, platform, and purpose. The acceptance of the mark of the beast will not be an inadvertent, casual, or accidental act. Those who receive it will make a deliberate choice to do so. They will know exactly what it means when they choose to accept it.

Second, the mark will provide an economic benefit to those who take it. The mark will become a person's ticket or passport for business. It will be required for all commercial transactions during the last half of the Tribulation (Revelation 13:17). This will help make a global order possible and will prevent the participation of anyone who refuses the mark. What's more, we can know that the mark is literal and visible, for it cannot serve as a ticket for commercial transactions if it's invisible.

Take a moment to think about this. It has been the dream of every tyrant down through history to so totally control his subjects that he alone decides who can buy or sell. When the beast or Antichrist seizes global power at the midpoint of the Tribulation, every person on earth will be faced with a monumental decision. Will he take the mark of the beast on his right hand or forehead, or will he refuse the mark and face death? Will he receive the mark that is required for every private and public transaction, or will he stand firm and say no to Antichrist?

The Antichrist's economic policy will be very simple: Take my mark and worship me, or starve. He will force people to make a

spiritual decision. They can either serve the Antichrist and worship the beast and his image, or they can refuse the Antichrist and
starve or face beheading. And only those who reject the beast will
know eternal life, whereas all who take the mark of the beast will
face the eternal judgment of God. Taking the mark will seal their
everlasting doom. It will be an unpardonable, irreversible sin:

> Another angel, a third one, followed them, saying with
> a loud voice, "If anyone worships the beast and his im-
> age, and receives a mark on his forehead or on his hand,
> he also will drink of the wine of the wrath of God, which
> is mixed in full strength in the cup of His anger; and he
> will be tormented with fire and brimstone in the pres-
> ence of the holy angels and in the presence of the Lamb.
> And the smoke of their torment goes up forever and ever;
> they have no rest day and night, those who worship the
> beast and his image, and whoever receives the mark of
> the name" (Revelation 14:9-10).

This reveals that a person's acceptance of the mark is not ultimately about economics. God does not condemn people for
purely economic reasons. Rather, He will judge those who choose
to receive the mark as a result of a conscious, deliberate decision
to worship the beast. It is the worship of the beast that will incur
God's wrath.

Does modern technology have anything to do with the mark of the beast?

What exactly will this mark be? What will it look like? What
form will it take? The speculation about this is almost endless.
Almost every new form of technology that has come along in recent decades has been related in one way or another to the mark

of the beast. Will the mark be something as simple as a tattoo? Will it be some kind of national ID card? Will it be a computer chip placed under the skin? Will it be some kind of bar code implanted on the right hand or the forehead?

In the aftermath of the terrorist attacks upon the World Trade Center and the Pentagon on 9/11, many people called for some form of a national ID card, a biometric identification system (which works via a thumbprint or an eye scan), or a digitized scanner technology to be put into place.[57] People feared the possibility of additional attacks and even talked about whether everyone should willingly give up certain freedoms so we can more easily apprehend those who might attempt future terrorist acts. Some have speculated that one of these new technologies might end up becoming the mark of the beast. Speculation has run rampant for years—the mark has been associated with Social Security numbers, bar code scanners, retina scanners, new chip implant technologies, and just about every other kind of new identification technology that comes along. There have been all kinds of unwarranted conjectures on the exact nature of the mark of the beast. As my friend Dr. Harold Willmington has said, "There's been a lot of sick, sick, sick about six, six, six."

When it comes to what the mark will look like or what form it will take, the answer is that we just don't know yet, and we shouldn't waste time thinking about it. We can know with certainty that nothing we see today is the mark of the beast. And we don't know what method Antichrist will adopt to implement this mark upon his worshipers. The text of Revelation 13:16 clearly indicates that the mark will be placed "on" the right hand or forehead, not *in* it. That is, the mark will be placed on the *outside* of a person's skin, where it can be seen. The Greek preposition *epi,* in this context, means "upon."

What we can safely and responsibly say is that the technology is certainly available today to tattoo, brand, or partially embed a visible identifying number or mark on the skin of every person alive for the purpose of regulating world commerce and controlling people's lives. While none of the things we see today are the mark of the beast, the rise of amazing new means of locating, identifying, and controlling people's lives strikingly foreshadows the scenario depicted in Revelation 13. It's just another indicator that points toward the picture Scripture paints of the end times.

One other point here bears mention. As amazing as the idea of the mark of the beast is, there's something much more stunning to be noticed here that we dare not miss. The Bible predicted this world economic system and identifying mark 1900 years ago. The fact that the words of Revelation 13 were penned in the age of wood, stones, swords, and spears makes this prophecy one of the most powerful proofs of the inspired nature and reliability of God's Word that one could imagine. Who could have predicted a one-world economic system that controls all commerce but God? As God says, "I am God, and there is no other; I am God, and there is no one like Me, declaring the end from the beginning, and from ancient times things which have not been done" (Isaiah 46:9-10). This astounding prophecy is just one more compelling piece of evidence that the God of the Bible is the true and living God and that the Bible is His inspired, inerrant Word.

How will the Antichrist persuade people to take the mark?

I don't know if you've ever thought about this before, but I've often wondered how the Antichrist will be able to pull off the 666 scheme. After all, most people—even those who have little or no biblical knowledge—have heard about 666 and know that it's associated with evil. There are an astounding number of Web sites devoted to the mysterious mark. Anyone who has seen popular movies like *The Omen* or has even a passing interest in rock music has heard of 666 and its association with the Antichrist. The point is that people everywhere know something about 666.

That being the case, how will the Antichrist convince billions of people to receive the mark on their bodies? Surely he would be shrewd enough to use 665 or 667 or any number besides the notorious 666.

One possible scenario is that the Antichrist will be so bold, blasphemous, and arrogant that he will be able to use his charisma and mesmerizing oratory to convince people to take this taboo mark. Though people will know that accepting the mark is an affront to God, they will take it anyway as a sign of open rebellion against the one true God.

A second possible answer is that the Antichrist may use the rapture of the church—the disappearance of millions of people—to play on people's fears. He may claim to be the only one on earth who knows the explanation for what happened to all the people who were raptured. He may even claim to have caused the disappearances and threaten those who rebel against him that they will disappear too. He may issue some kind of promise that no more people will disappear or be "vaporized" provided they register themselves to take his mark. That may explain how he gets the whole world to unite under his political, economic, and religious system.

Another possible explanation is found in the chilling words of 2 Thessalonians 2:9-11, where the apostle Paul described the rampant deception that will flood the earth during the end times:

The one whose coming is in accord with the activity of

Satan, with all power and signs and false wonders, and with all the deception of wickedness for those who perish, because they did not receive the love of the truth so as to be saved. For this reason God will send upon them a deluding influence so that they will believe what is false, in order that they all may be judged who did not believe the truth, but took pleasure in wickedness.

What this means is that during the coming Tribulation the Antichrist will be empowered by Satan to perform incredible signs and wonders that will amaze and dumbfound even sophisticated modern mankind. His deception will create awe and wonder that will draw billions of people to turn to him as a savior. Those who turn from the truth of God to Antichrist and refuse God's gracious offer of salvation will be turned over to their own self-willed choice. God will confirm their choice and send a deluding influence on them so that they will receive, literally, "the lie." What is the lie? The belief that the Antichrist is God. This means that even though people will have knowledge about 666 and its evil connotations, they will gladly accept the mark and all it represents. The strong delusion will overcome any hesitation they might have about taking the mark of the beast. That so many will choose to follow Antichrist—and subsequent eternal condemnation—should lead us all to make sure we know where we stand with the Lord. Times of powerful delusion are coming.

10 Keys to Understanding the Mark of the Beast

1. The mark is future, not past.
2. The mark is a literal, visible brand, mark, or tattoo.

3. It will be placed "on" the right hand or forehead of people during the Tribulation.

4. The mark will be given as a sign of devotion to Antichrist and as a passport to engage in commerce.

5. The mark will be the number 666, or the numerical value of the Antichrist's name.

6. Those who are believers will be able to calculate the number and identify the Antichrist.

7. Those who take the mark will be eternally doomed.

8. Before the rapture, no one should attempt to identify the Antichrist or his mark.

9. While current technology and methods of identifying and locating people strikingly foreshadow the possible means by which the Antichrist will attempt to control the world, no specific technology presently in existence should be identified as the mark of the beast. No one can say specifically what technology will be employed to fulfill this prophecy, but what we see today certainly makes such a system not only possible, but probable.

10. In spite of 666's association with evil, the number will be received by those who willfully reject Christ during the Tribulation.

PART 3

The Coming of the Antichrist

———————o———————

*"We do not want another committee, we have too many
already. What we want is a man of sufficient stature to hold
the allegiance of all the people and to lift us up out of the
economic morass into which we are sinking. Send us such a
man, and whether he be God or devil, we will receive him."*

PAUL HENRI SPAAK
(FIRST PRESIDENT OF THE UNITED NATIONS GENERAL ASSEMBLY
AND A KEY PLANNER IN THE FORMATION OF THE
EUROPEAN ECONOMIC COMMUNITY IN 1957)

*"The time comes, it is quite clear.
The Antichrist is very near."*

SEBASTIAN BRANT
THE SHIP OF FOOLS, CIII. 92-93

How will the Antichrist rise to world power?

This is one of the more challenging questions to answer about
the Antichrist. How will a man like this rise to power? What could
possibly lead well-educated and sophisticated people to turn to a
leader like the Antichrist? And ultimately to worship him as God?
Of course, in asking these questions, we have to remember that

only a few decades ago an entire nation came under the spell of a vicious, murderous madman named Adolf Hitler. So it's not like such an occurrence is without modern precedent.

While no one knows the exact details of how his rise will be orchestrated, everyone knows that our world today is desperately looking for leadership. In the face of mounting international crises, the world is looking for someone with the charisma, leadership, and savvy to bring the world together to meet these critical challenges.

One of the chronic problems the world faces is the perpetual Middle East conflict, which has given rise to what appears to be a never-ending and ill-named "peace process." Solving the Middle East crisis is undoubtedly the most coveted prize in the history of international diplomacy. The world is clamoring for peace. Every leader wants to be the one who adds this victory to the resume of his accomplishments, and the Bible says that the Antichrist will pull it off. He will make his debut on the world scene by forging some kind of agreement or treaty with the nation of Israel. Daniel 9:27 provides the details:

> He will make a firm covenant with the many for one week, but in the middle of the week he will put a stop to sacrifice and grain offering; and on the wing of abominations will come one who makes desolate, even until a complete destruction, one that is decreed, is poured out on the one who makes desolate.

What is the exact nature of this covenant that Antichrist will make with Israel? While the above passage doesn't specifically tell us the exact nature of this treaty, we can easily read between the lines. Charles Dyer, a respected prophecy teacher and author, says,

What is this "covenant" that the Antichrist will make with Israel? Daniel does not specify its content, but he does indicate that it will extend for seven years. During the first half of this time Israel feels at peace and secure, so the covenant must provide some guarantee for Israel's national security. Very likely the covenant will allow Israel to be at peace with her Arab neighbors. One result of the covenant is that Israel will be allowed to rebuild her temple in Jerusalem. This world ruler will succeed where Kissinger, Carter, Reagan, Bush, and other world leaders have failed. He will be known as the man of peace![1]

That there will be a time of peace for Israel in the end times, at least temporarily, is confirmed by Ezekiel 38:8,11,14:

After many days you will be summoned; in the latter years you will come into the land that is restored from the sword, whose inhabitants have been gathered from many nations to the mountains of Israel which had been a continual waste; but its people were brought out from the nations, and they are living securely, all of them... and you will say, "I will go up against the land of un-walled villages. I will go against those who are at rest, that live securely, all of them living without walls and having no bars or gates."...Therefore prophesy, son of man, and say to Gog, "Thus says the Lord GOD, 'On that day when My people Israel are living securely, will you not know it?'"

Other Bible passages indicate that commencement of the Tribulation, the entire world will enjoy a season of peace brokered by the Antichrist:

1 Thessalonians 5:1-3

Now as to the times and the epochs, brethren, you have no need of anything to be written to you. For you yourselves know full well that the day of the Lord will come just like a thief in the night. While they are saying, "Peace and safety!" then destruction will come upon them suddenly like labor pains upon a woman with child, and they will not escape.

Revelation 6:1-2

I saw when the Lamb broke one of the seven seals, and I heard one of the four living creatures saying as with a voice of thunder, "Come." I looked, and behold, a white horse, and he who sat on it had a bow; and a crown was given to him, and he went out conquering and to conquer.

It's clear that the breaking of the first seal brings peace because the breaking of the second seal, which brings forth the rider on the red horse, brings an end to that peace. Revelation 6:3-4 goes on to say, "When He [Christ] broke the second seal, I heard the second living creature saying, 'Come.' And another, a red horse, went out; and to him who sat on it, it was granted to take peace from the earth, and that men would slay one another; and a great sword was given to him." Obviously, the rider on the red horse can't take peace from the earth if there isn't any peace already in place. The Antichrist, the rider on the white horse, will bring the world what it has always wanted. W.A. Criswell, the former pastor of First Baptist Church of Dallas, looks ahead to that day:

In a day of revolution, in a day of chaos, in a day of storm and fury, comes this great and final ruler. That is the meaning of the opening of the first seal in Revelation 6. In keeping with the opening of the first seal, chapter 17 of the Apocalypse says that those ten kings willingly, with one mind, gave to him their power, their strength and their authority. When the first seal is opened, this final anti-Christ appears. He comes riding a white horse, with a bow and no arrows. He comes conquering and to conquer, but he is a bloodless conqueror. There is no war, there is no battle, there is no resistance. In the midst of their chaos and despair, these kings of the earth, the rulers of the earth, gladly yield to him and they hail him as the savior of the race. They say: "This is the man who can lead us out, this is the man who has the answer to our questions, this is the man who can bring peace and prosperity to all mankind. All hail!" The people will be attracted to him and wonder will turn into worship. This is the great and final ruler of the earth.[2]

The Antichrist will rise to power as a great man of peace. I don't know how you envision the Antichrist, but most people probably think of a crazed, diabolical fiend—a shameless megalomaniac. All of these images are accurate, but none of them pictures what he will be like when the world gets its first impression of him. At the commencement of his career he will rise to prominence as the popular peacemaker. The prolific problem solver. The distinguished diplomat. He will arrive on the world stage with an olive branch in his hand. John MacArthur aptly describes the world situation that will give rise to the Antichrist:

> In the chaotic times of confusion, uncertainty, and unrest that will prevail during the Tribulation, the world will long for a leader. People will be desperately hoping

for someone powerful and influential to unite the divided and contentious nations of the world; someone to bring hope in the midst of hopelessness; someone to provide a sense of security in an unsettled time of apprehension and fear. People will be desperately seeking a strong, charismatic, authoritative leader to pull the world back from the brink of disaster. These longings will be fulfilled. The powerful leader people will desire will come and unify the world under his rule. He will appear at first to be everything people thought they were looking for. And for a brief time he will bring peace and prosperity. But he will turn out to be far more than the world bargained for. He will be a dictator more cruel- and powerful than any other leader the world has ever known. This man, often called the Antichrist, will be the culmination of a long line of would-be conquerors. What men like Alexander the Great and the Roman emperors in ancient times and Hitler and Stalin in modern times only dreamed of doing, the Antichrist will actually do—he will rule the entire world and receive its worship.[3]

The world stage is already set for his coming. The signs all point toward his entrance in the not-too-distant future.

What are some of the signs of his coming?

One thing is clear about the rise of Antichrist: It can't occur in a vacuum. The stage must be set for his coming. What are some of the necessary preconditions for his rise, according to Scripture? I've listed here five signs that are predicted in the Bible. All five, by the way, are very much a part of today's news headlines, which indicates that the Antichrist's appearance could very well take place anytime soon.

The Regathering of Israel

Almost all the key events of the end times hinge in one way or another on the existence of the nation of Israel. Israel is the battleground for all the great end-time wars and conflicts described in the Bible (Ezekiel 38; Zechariah 12). The people of this nation must be preserved and regathered to their ancient homeland before end-time biblical prophecies can be fulfilled. The last days will officially begin when the Antichrist makes a seven-year treaty with Israel (Daniel 9:27). Obviously, for this to happen, Israel must exist. The Antichrist can't establish a treaty with the Jewish people unless they comprise a recognized nation. Before 1948, when the modern state of Israel was founded, this prophecy regarding a treaty could not have been fulfilled. But with Israel now an established nation within the world community, this piece of the end-time puzzle is now in place.

The fact that the Jewish people have remained a distinct people for almost 2000 years and have regathered and become a nation in their ancient homeland is truly astounding. Dr. Randall Price highlights the modern miracle of the Jewish people:

> The modern return of the Jewish people to the Land of Israel has been called the "Miracle on the Mediterranean." Such a return by a people group that had been scattered among the nations is unprecedented in history. Indeed, the Jewish people are the only exiled people to remain a distinct people despite being dispersed to more than 70 different countries for more than 20 centuries. The mighty empires of Egypt, Assyria, Babylon, Persia, Greece, and Rome all ravaged their land, took their people captive, and scattered them throughout the earth. Even after this, they suffered persecution, pogrom, and Holocaust in the lands to which they were exiled. Yet, all

of these ancient kingdoms have turned to dust and their former glories remain only as museum relics and many of the nations that opposed the Jews have suffered economic, political, or religious decline. But the Jewish people whom they enslaved and tried to eradicate live free and have again become a strong nation![4]

And not only have the Jewish people survived as a distinct people down through the centuries, they have also been restored to their ancient homeland against staggering odds. They have also even revived their dead language:

> The fact of the Jewish people's continuity is even more remarkable in light of the testimony of history to exile and return. In all of human history there have been less than ten deportations of a people group from their native land. These people groups disappeared in history because they assimilated into the nations to which they were exiled. However, the Jewish people did not simply experience a single exile, but multiple exiles...The contrast here with other historical exiles should not be overlooked. While other people groups were exiled to one country, the Jews were dispersed to many different countries, and in fact were scattered to every part of the earth. The Jewish people also hold the distinction of being the only people to have successfully revived their ancient tongue after more than 2,000 years. In the late 19th century, when Jews began immigration to the Land, Jews only spoke the languages of the countries from which they had returned. One man, Eliezer Ben-Yehuda, decided that the proper tongue for the Jewish people who were now back in the land of the prophets was the language of the prophets. He began teaching the children, and today

Hebrew is spoken daily by every man, woman, and child in Israel. By contrast, what country or people group today speak Egyptian, Assyrian, or Latin? Only the Jewish people have successfully regained the use of their original language in everyday life...Moreover, the Jewish people are the only people to have returned *en masse* to their ancient homeland and to have restored their national independence by re-establishing their former state...Any one of these facts of Israel's survival would be remarkable, but taken together they are miraculous.[5]

In God's perfect timing, just as the Bible predicted about 2500 years ago, the Jewish people are continuing to be restored to their land from all over the earth. We have a front-row seat to watching this miracle happen. This critical cog of end-time prophecy is now in place. The gears are beginning to turn, and the rise of Antichrist may not be far behind.

The Reuniting of the Roman Empire

It's been noted several times in this book that the Antichrist will rise from a reunited Roman Empire. While nothing we see today comprises the final form of the reunited or revived Roman Empire specifically under the rule of ten kings (the Group of Ten), the stirrings that have taken place in Europe since the end of WW II are astounding. In the wake of two crippling world wars, the nations of Europe have come to recognize that their only hope for survival and stability rest in setting up some kind of peaceful alliance. Beginning in 1957, that coalition began to form. Here's a brief overview of how that coalition has grown from a loose association of 6 nations into a global powerhouse of 27 nations with a 736-member parliament and a population of half a billion.

An Overview of the
Reuniting of Europe

Birth of the modern EU (Treaty of Rome) with   1957
6 nations: Belgium, Germany, Luxembourg,
France, Italy, and the Netherlands
(total of 220 million people).

EEC (European Economic Community) is   1973
formed; Denmark, Ireland, and Great Britain
join, adding 66 million more people.

Greece joins the EEC, becoming the tenth   1981
member.

Portugal and Spain join the EEC.   1986

Official formation of the EU, and signing   February 7, 1992
of the Maastricht Treaty takes place.

Austria, Finland, and Sweden join the EU,   1995
bringing the total population to 362 million in
15 member nations.

Formation of the Monetary Union of the EU   January 1, 1999
takes place, designating a new shared currency
called the euro.

Euro currency officially issued (known as   January 1, 2002
e-day).

In the shadow of the ancient acropolis in   April 16, 2004
Athens, Greece, 10 more nations sign treaties
to join the EU: Cyprus, the Czech Republic,
Estonia, Hungary, Latvia, Lithuania, Malta,
Poland, Slovakia, and Slovenia. The population
of the EU was raised to almost half a billion.

The 25 member nations of the EU sign the new EU Constitution, amid great pomp, at a ceremony on Capitoline Hill in Rome.	October 29, 2004
Romanian and Bulgaria join, bringing the total number of nations to 27.	2007
Lisbon Treaty is ratified (established a permanent office of "president of Europe" with a 2½ year term).	December 1, 2009

This new alignment of power points toward the revived Roman Empire and its new leader, who will bring the promise of peace to a world that will be teetering on the brink of catastrophe and chaos. I believe we are witnessing the embryonic stages of the emergence of an increasingly unified and powerful Roman Empire, just as Bible prophecy tells us to expect in the last days. As prophecy scholars Thomas Ice and Timothy Demy aptly conclude,

> One would have to be totally ignorant of developments within the world of our day not to admit that, through the efforts of the European Union, "Humpty Dumpty" is finally being put back together again. This is occurring, like all of the other needed developments of prophecy, at just the right time to be in place for the coming tribulation period.[6]

Globalism

The scene today is ripe for an international economy and eventually a global government. In the wake of the brutal economic disaster that occurred in late 2008 and early 2009—which was felt globally and is still being felt in late 2010 as I write this—the leaders of the world gathered to come up with strategies for staving off a complete economic collapse and establishing some kind of economic road map for the future. Calls for a new world order were heard from Great Britain all the way across the Atlantic Ocean to the United States. The growing consensus among world leaders seems to be that only a consolidation and concentration of power will save the globe from economic disaster and self-destruction. That's the kind of scenario envisioned in Scripture at the time the Antichrist steps onto the world scene. In a very short period of time, he will take control of the world economy and seize the reins of political power.

The Rebuilt Temple

According to the Bible, a third Jewish Temple, often known as the Tribulation Temple, must be built on the 35-acre Temple Mount in Jerusalem. The first Jewish Temple was built by Solomon and was destroyed in 586 BC by the Babylonians. The second Temple was built by Zerubbabel and greatly embellished by Herod the Great. It was reduced to rubble in AD 70 by the Romans.

The Bible indicates in at least four places that the Jewish people will build a third Temple on the Temple Mount, and they will do so in the end times.

Daniel 9:27	"He [Antichrist] will make a firm covenant with the many for one week, but in the middle of the week he will put a stop to sacrifice and grain offering."
Matthew 24:15	"When you see the abomination of desolation which was spoken of through Daniel the prophet, standing in the holy place..."

2 Thessalonians 2:4	"[He] opposes and exalts himself above every so-called god or object of worship, so that he takes his seat in the temple of God, displaying himself as being God."
Revelation 11:1-2	"There was given to me a measuring rod like a staff; and someone said, 'Get up and measure the temple of God and the altar, and those who worship in it. And leave out the court which is outside the temple, and do not measure it, for it has been given to the nations; and they will tread under foot the holy city for forty-two months.'"

We know that this third Temple has to be built before Antichrist rises to power because he will make a treaty with the Jewish people that evidently gives them access to the Temple so they can reinstitute and carry out the sacrificial system (Daniel 9:27). Also, 2 Thessalonians 2:4 says that the Antichrist will sit in the Temple and declare that he is God.

This brings us to one of the thorniest problems in all of Bible prophecy: How can the Jews rebuild their Temple when the Muslim Dome of the Rock and Al-Aqsa mosque are standing in the way? As things stand now, it looks impossible for the Temple to ever be rebuilt on the site. But we should never forget that before 1948, many people thought it was impossible for the Jewish people to ever be restored to their ancient homeland. Yet today almost 40 percent of the Jewish people in the world now live in Israel. And incredibly, almost two-thirds of them want to see the Temple rebuilt.

Ynetnews reported the startling findings of a new poll about the Temple on July 30, 2009. The poll asked respondents whether they wanted to see the Temple rebuilt:

Sixty-four percent responded favorably, while 36% said no. An analysis of the answers showed that not only the ultra-Orthodox and the religious look forward to the rebuilding of the Temple (100% and 97% respectively), but also the traditional public (91%) and many seculars—47%…The Temple was destroyed 1,942 years ago, and almost two-thirds of the population want to see it rebuilt, including 47% of seculars.

This groundswell of support for the building of the third Jewish Temple is a key sign of the times. For years, groups like the Temple Mount Faithful and others have championed and even made preparations for the rebuilding of the Temple, but broad public support was woefully lacking. That appears to have changed. Today, there are many in Israel who want the Temple built. And it must be in place during the Tribulation period so the sacrificial system can be reinstituted and the Antichrist can take his seat in the Temple and defile it. While no one knows when the Temple will be rebuilt or what circumstances will make this possible, the level of support for the rebuilding effort is rising rapidly, which serves as yet another sign that the last days are approaching.

Randall Price, the foremost evangelical Christian authority on the Temple, concludes his excellent book *The Coming Last Days Temple* with these words:

> What does this say to you and me? It says that not only have the Jews already begun the ascent to their goal, but they are only one step away from accomplishing it! As this book has shown, the current conflict over the Temple Mount and the resolve of the Jewish activists to prepare for the conclusion of this conflict have provided the

momentum for the short distance that remains of the climb. We live in a day that is on the brink of the rebuilding effort, and with it the beginning of the fulfillment of the prophecies that will move the world rapidly to see as a reality the coming Last Days Temple.[7]

Two of the key events that must occur before the Temple can be rebuilt have already occurred: The Jews are back in their land, and they have control of Jerusalem. All that remains is for them to have sovereignty over the Temple Mount itself and for something to happen to the Muslim Dome of the Rock. When God brings these events to fruition—which He will, in His time—the Temple will be rebuilt. And Antichrist's desolation of it won't be far behind. Events taking place today are paving the way for these prophecies to be fulfilled.

World Outcry for Peace

"It is a riddle wrapped up in a mystery inside an enigma."

In a speech broadcast on October 1, 1939, that's how Sir Winston Churchill described the actions of the Russians in his day. And what he said about Russia's actions could be applied to the Middle East today. After all, what's the number one problem in the world today? The persistent Middle East crisis: Israel versus the Palestinians, Israel versus Hezbollah, Israel versus Iran. The tiny nation of Israel is in the crosshairs of the Islamic nations that surround her. Since 1948, one U.S. presidential administration after another has tried to solve this enigma, and while there have been brief, shallow victories and times of no war, a real and lasting peace has consistently eluded the world's most skilled diplomats. But the Bible indicates all that will dramatically change someday.

As the head of a multinational confederation, the Antichrist will apparently have the power and skill to initiate, formulate, and impose a peace covenant on Israel and possibly her neighbors.[8] Concerning the nature of this peace treaty, prophecy scholar John Walvoord said,

> When a Gentile ruler over the ten nations imposes a peace treaty on Israel, it will be from superior strength and will not be a negotiated peace treaty, but it apparently will include the necessary elements for such a contract. It will include the fixing of Israel's borders, the establishment of trade relations with her neighbors— something she does not enjoy at the present time, and, most of all, it will provide protection from outside attacks, which will allow Israel to relax her military preparedness. It can also be anticipated that some attempts will be made to open the holy areas of Jerusalem to all faiths related to it.[9]

The idea of a peace imposed upon Israel by a confederation of Western nations seems like a very probable scenario today. One can easily see in today's environment how the Antichrist could come on the scene and compel Israel to accept an imposed peace—a take-it-or-leave-it deal. After all, the world is growing more and more frustrated with the worsening situation in the Middle East. Many are running low on patience. A forced peace by a powerful leader could certainly fit with what Bible prophecy says will happen in the last days.

In summary, events taking place in our world today seem to indicate that Antichrist's arrival may occur soon. Let's recap the evidence we've looked at:

Key Biblical Clues for Antichrist's Rise	The World Stage Today
The Antichrist will rise from a reunited Roman Empire at a time when it's ruled by ten leaders.	The European Union is now firmly in place. It is not currently ruled over by the "Group of Ten," but the basic form has taken shape.
The Antichrist will rise on a platform of peace for the Middle East.	The Middle East crisis is the number one international problem in the world today.
The Antichrist will sit in the rebuilt Temple in Jerusalem and declare he is God.	Israel became a nation in May 1948 and seized control of Jerusalem in June 1967. There is now a growing movement to rebuild the Temple.
The Antichrist will rule the entire world politically, economically, and religiously.	Globalism or globalization is a present reality. In fact, in our current world climate, it's a necessity.
The Antichrist will force all people to take his mark of allegiance to survive.	The technology that makes it possible to do something like this already exists, but we don't know the specifics of how this will be done or carried out.

Pastor and author David Jeremiah summarizes how world conditions today are ripe for the Antichrist's coming:

> Today it is much easier to envision the possibility of such a world ruler. Technology has given us instant global communications. CNN is seen everywhere in the world. The Internet and satellite cell phones reach every country on the face of the earth. Air transportation has

shrunk the planet to the point where we can set foot on the soil of any nation in a matter of hours. I am told there are now missiles that can reach any part of the world in fewer than thirty minutes. Men and nations no longer live in isolation. There are also other factors that make the ascendance of a global leader more plausible than ever before. The Bible predicts that worldwide chaos, instability, and disorder will increase as we approach the end of this age...Just before these tensions explode into world chaos, the Rapture of the church will depopulate much of the planet...The devastation wrought by these disasters will spur a worldwide outcry for relief and order at almost any cost. That will set the stage for the emergence of a new world leader who will, like a pied piper, promise a solution to all problems.[10]

PART 4

The Career of the Antichrist

---○---

*"The world has a death-wish to be
dominated by the Antichrist."*

FATHER VINCENT MICELI
THE ANTICHRIST (1981)

What will the Antichrist do during his career?

The career of the Antichrist will rise and fall much like a Roman candle lit up on the Fourth of July. He will start out with great fanfare and streak brightly across the skyline of world politics and economics. Then he will explode in a great burst of power and dominion for three-and-a-half years. And at the end, he will fizzle out under the withering judgment of Christ at His second coming. His career, while brief, will be filled with stunning successes and staggering setbacks. The world will have never seen anyone like him. While we do not know all of what will take place during his short time in power, the Bible does provide some details about his activities:

The Antichrist's Activities

1. He will appear in "the time of the end" of Israel's history (Daniel 8:17).

2. His manifestation will signal the beginning of the day of the Lord (2 Thessalonians 2:1-3).

3. His unveiling is currently being hindered by "what restrains him now" (2 Thessalonians 2:3-7).

4. His rise to power will come through peace programs (Revelation 6:2). He will make a covenant of peace with Israel (Daniel 9:27). This event will signal the beginning of the seven-year Tribulation. He will later break that covenant at its midpoint.

5. Near the middle of the Tribulation, the Antichrist will be assassinated or violently killed (Revelation 13:3,12,14).

6. He will "come up out of the abyss" (Revelation 17:8).

7. He will be raised back to life (Revelation 11:7; 13:3,12,14; 17:8).

8. The whole world will be amazed and will follow after him (Revelation 13:3).

9. He will be totally controlled and energized by Satan (Revelation 13:2-5).

10. He will assassinate three of the ten kings in the reunited Roman Empire (Daniel 7:24).

11. The kings will give all authority to the beast (Revelation 17:12-13).

12. He will invade the land of Israel and desecrate the rebuilt Temple (Daniel 9:27; 11:41; 12:11; Matthew 24:15; Revelation 11:2).

13. He will mercilessly pursue and persecute the Jewish people (Daniel 7:21,25; Revelation 12:6).

14. He will set himself up in the Temple as God (2 Thessalonians 2:4).

15. He will be worshiped as God for three-and-a-half years (Revelation 13:4-8). His claim to deity will be accompanied by great signs and wonders (2 Thessalonians 2:9-12).

16. He will speak great blasphemies against God (Daniel 7:8; Revelation 13:6).

17. He will rule the world politically, religiously, and economically for three-and-a-half years (Revelation 13:4-8,16-18).

18. He will be promoted by a second beast who will lead the world in worship of the beast (Revelation 13:11-18).

19. He will require all to receive his mark (666) before they can buy and sell (Revelation 13:16-18).

20. He will establish his political and economic capital in Babylon (Revelation 17).

21. He and the ten kings will destroy Babylon (Revelation 18:16).

22. He will kill the two witnesses (Revelation 11:7).

23. He will gather all the nations against Jerusalem (Zechariah 12:1-2; 14:1-3; Revelation 16:16; 19:19).

24. He will fight against Christ when He returns to earth and will suffer total defeat (Revelation 19:19).

25. He will be cast alive into the lake of fire (Daniel 7:11; Revelation 19:20).

How long will he rule the world?

According to Scripture, the worldwide kingdom of the Antichrist will last for three-and-a-half years. He will undoubtedly be on the world scene as a key player for several years leading up to his seizure of power, but we have no idea how long he will have to wait in the wings. His rise will appear insignificant at first, for Daniel 7:8 describes him as a "little horn." But he will eventually become a world ruler, and his kingdom will last a brief three-and-a-half years. This three-and-a-half-year period is stated in various ways in the Scripture, but it always equals the same length of time.

42 months   Revelation 11:2; 13:5

time, times, and half a time   Daniel 7:25; 12:7;
(time = one year, times = two years, Revelation 12:14
half a time = half a year)

1260 days   Revelation 11:3; 12:6
(using the 360-day calendar, 1260
days = three-and-a-half years)

The Antichrist will set up his worldwide kingdom in a futile attempt to preempt the coming kingdom of Jesus Christ. But Christ will come in great power and glory at His second advent to destroy the Antichrist and establish His earthly kingdom, which will last 1000 years.

What is the Antichrist's relationship to Babylon?

Revelation 13 unveils the end-time empire of the Antichrist as enveloping the global political, economic, and religious realms. Revelation 17 gives a further description of his reign and discloses the close connection between the beast and Babylon. Some have called this account "beauty on the beast."

> He carried me away in the Spirit into a wilderness; and I saw a woman sitting on a scarlet beast, full of blasphemous names, having seven heads and ten horns. The woman was clothed in purple and scarlet, and adorned with gold and precious stones and pearls, having in her hand a gold cup full of abominations and of the unclean things of her immorality, and on her forehead a name was written, a mystery, "BABYLON THE GREAT, THE MOTHER OF HARLOTS AND OF THE ABOMINATIONS OF THE EARTH."...The woman whom you saw is the great city, which reigns over the kings of the earth (verses 3-5,18).

During the end times, things will come full circle from the ancient Tower of Babel. In Genesis 10–11, the world's first powerful leader, Nimrod, built a great city (Babylon) and an evil religious system to go along with it. Babylon, in Genesis, was both a city and a system. In Revelation 17–18, Babylon is again mentioned as a great city and a religious-commercial system all wrapped up in one, and the city and the beast are closely associated with one another. Babylon, pictured as a brazen prostitute, rides on the back of the beast, or the Antichrist. This probably indicates that the beast supports the woman while she initially exercises some control over him. In other words, they will be very closely connected and dependent upon each other.

But what is Babylon? While many believe that Babylon (in the book of Revelation) is a kind of code name for Rome, or New York City, or some other great end-time city, I believe it refers to a literal rebuilt city of Babylon on the Euphrates River in modern-day Iraq that will serve as a political headquarters for the

Antichrist. This is the view presented in the popular Left Behind series written by Tim LaHaye and Jerry Jenkins. In the first book, *Left Behind,* this conversation appears:

> "He wants to move the U.N."…
> "Where?"…
> "He wants to move it to Babylon."…
> "I hear they've been renovating that city for years. Millions of dollars invested in making it, what, New Babylon?"
> "Billions."…
> "Within a year the United Nations headquarters will move to New Babylon."[1]

In the novel, the Antichrist, Nicolae Carpathia, moves the United Nations and his world headquarters to the rebuilt city of Babylon, called New Babylon, which is located on the Euphrates River in Iraq. While *Left Behind* is fiction, this breathtaking event, the rise of New Babylon, is based on ancient biblical prophecies that as of yet are unfulfilled.

There are several reasons for my conviction that Babylon will be a literal, rebuilt city, and I'll give a few of the key ones here. First, "Babylon" appears almost 300 times in the Bible, and with one possible exception in 1 Peter 5:13, the name always refers to a literal city of Babylon in what is now known as Iraq. The great end-time city of Antichrist is referred to as "Babylon" six times in Revelation (14:8; 16:19; 17:5; 18:2,10,21). Because the term "Revelation" (Greek = *apokalupsis*) in Revelation 1:1 refers to something that is revealed or unveiled, it would be strange to interpret "Babylon" literally everywhere else in the Bible, but then suddenly insist upon a symbolic meaning when "Babylon" appears in the last book of Scripture.

Second, the other geographical locations mentioned in Revelation are understood literally. This includes Patmos, Ephesus,

Smyrna, Pergamum, Thyatira, Sardis, Philadelphia, Laodicea, Armageddon, and the New Jerusalem. If all these places are understood in a literal sense, why not accept Babylon in a literal sense as well? As Henry Morris notes, "In the absence of any statement in the context to the contrary, therefore, we must assume that the term Babylon applies to the real city of Babylon, although it also may extend far beyond that to the whole system centered at Babylon as well."[2]

Third, the Bible repeatedly predicts that Babylon will experience a cataclysmic, sudden destruction, but that has never happened yet. For example, Isaiah 13:4-5 says, "A sound of tumult on the mountains, like that of many people! A sound of the uproar of kingdoms, of nations gathered together! The LORD of hosts is mustering the army for battle. They are coming from a far country, from the farthest horizons, the LORD and His instruments of indignation, to destroy the whole land."

Isaiah continues in 13:10-13:

> The stars of heaven and their constellations will not flash forth their light; the sun will be dark when it rises and the moon will not shed its light. Thus I will punish the world for its evil and the wicked for their iniquity; I will also put an end to the arrogance of the proud and abase the haughtiness of the ruthless. I will make mortal man scarcer than pure gold and mankind than the gold of Ophir. Therefore I will make the heavens tremble, and the earth will be shaken from its place at the fury of the LORD of hosts in the day of His burning anger.

In this chapter, it appears that the prophet Isaiah was looking down the corridor of time to the future destruction of Babylon in the last days, for nothing like this has happened to Babylon since that prophecy was uttered. Jesus even quoted Isaiah 13:10 in Matthew 24:29 when He described the stellar signs that will accompany His second coming to earth—a clear indication that Jesus saw the fulfillment of Isaiah 13:10 as still in the future.

Isaiah also seems to refer to the destruction of Babylon in connection with the second coming of Christ in Isaiah 13:20-22:

> [Babylon] will never be inhabited or lived in from generation to generation; nor will the Arab pitch his tent there, nor will shepherds make their flock lie down there. But desert creatures will lie down there, and their houses will be full of owls; ostriches also will live there, and shaggy goats will frolic there. Hyenas will howl in their fortified towers and jackals in their luxurious palaces. [Babylon's] fateful time also will soon come, and her days will not be prolonged.

Isaiah 13:19 even says that when Babylon is finally destroyed it will be "as when God overthrew Sodom and Gomorrah." The prophet Jeremiah says the same thing:

> Behold, she will be the least of the nations, a wilderness, a parched land and a desert. Because of the indignation of the LORD she will not be inhabited, but she will be completely desolate…Come to her from the farthest border; open up her barns, pile her up like heaps and utterly destroy her, let nothing be left to her…Therefore the desert creatures will live there along with the jackals; the ostriches also will live in it, and it will never again be inhabited or dwelt in from generation to generation. "As when God overthrew Sodom and Gomorrah with its neighbors," declares the LORD, "No man will live there, nor will any son of man reside in it" (Jeremiah 50:12-13,26,39-40).

As far as the historic fulfillment of these verses is concerned, it is obvious from both Scripture and history that hasn't yet occurred. I believe the literal fulfillment of that passage will take place during the end times, and it will happen to a rebuilt city of Babylon.

Fourth, Babylon is in a prime location today to dominate the Middle East, which is the world's cauldron for unrest as well as the home of almost two-thirds of the world's known oil reserves. Henry Morris highlights the advantages of Babylon as a world capital:

> Nevertheless, Babylon is indeed a prime prospect for rebuilding, entirely apart from any prophetic intimations. Its location is the most ideal in the world for any kind of international center. Not only is it in the beautiful and fertile Tigris-Euphrates plain, but it is near some of the world's richest oil reserves. Computer studies for the Institute of Creation Research have shown, for example, that Babylon is very near the geographical center of all the earth's land masses. It is within navigable distances to the Persian Gulf and is at the crossroads of the three great continents of Europe, Asia, and Africa. Thus there is no more ideal location anywhere for a world trade center, a world communications center, a world banking center, a world educational center, or especially a world capital! The greatest historian of modern times, Arnold Toynbee, used to stress to all his readers and hearers that Babylon would be the best place in the world to build a future world cultural metropolis. With all these advantages, and with the head start already made by the Iraqis, it is not far-fetched at all to suggest that the future capital of the "United Nations Kingdom" is the ten-nation federation.[3]

Just as many people in the past questioned how Israel would ever become a nation again, many people today wonder how Babylon could ever serve as a great headquarters for the Antichrist during the end times. Some also ask, "If Babylon has to be rebuilt, then how close can we really be to the coming of Christ? After all, it will take some time to rebuild Babylon and make it into the city described in Revelation 17–18." However, we have to remember that the rapture could happen today and the Tribulation might not start until several months or even several years later. The rapture is not the event that signals the beginning of the Tribulation. Rather, the Tribulation will commence when the Antichrist forges his peace treaty with Israel. There will undoubtedly be a time of further preparation or setting the stage between the rapture and the onset of the Tribulation. We have no idea how long that time will be, but it could be fairly extended. If so, that would help answer the questions about how quickly things might—or might not—fall into place after the rapture occurs.

Knowing what the Bible says about Babylon during the end times and its relationship to the coming world ruler, we shouldn't be surprised by all the attention the world has given to Iraq in recent decades. It's no accident that Iraq has come out of relative obscurity to play a significant role in world events. Also, the massive quantities of oil in Iraq—which can bring great wealth to the country—is not just a stroke of good fortune. God put the oil there. Iraq's place in the world spotlight could serve as a perfect prelude for the rebuilding of Babylon in the near future. The resurgence of Iraq, the efforts that have already been made to restore and rebuild Babylon, and the rich oil reserves available to finance the rebuilding of the city all make it very realistic for Babylon to serve as the end-times headquarters of the Antichrist.

Will he be assassinated and come back to life?

Several times in this book, I briefly mentioned the fact the Antichrist will die and come back to life. But will he really die and rise again? Or will it all be a hoax? The Bible text that describes this event is Revelation 13:3-4:

> I saw one of his heads as if it had been slain, and his fatal wound was healed. And the whole earth was amazed and followed after the beast; they worshiped the dragon because he gave his authority to the beast; and they worshiped the beast, saying, "Who is like the beast, and who is able to wage war with him?"

Revelation 17:8 is a parallel passage:

> The beast that you saw was, and is not, and is about to come up out of the abyss and go to destruction. And those who dwell on the earth, whose name has not been written in the book of life from the foundation of the world, will wonder when they see the beast, that he was and is not and will come.

There are three main views on the meaning of these texts. Some believe that the death and resurrection described here refers to the ending of the Roman Empire in AD 476 and its resuscitation in the end times. In other words, these passages are talking about the *empire* coming back to life, not a man.

Now, it is true that the beast in Revelation is both the empire and its emperor, the kingdom and its king. As we have often seen in history, a great leader at times can hardly be distinguished from his kingdom. Louis XIV is quoted as saying at one point, "I am France." The question here is which one is in view. It seems to me in Revelation 13:3-4 and 17:8 that the ruler of the empire is in view.

There are two key reasons to favor this view. First, the language in Revelation 13 appears, for the most part, to be referring to an individual. The pronouns "he" and "his" are used repeatedly. And the second beast, according to Revelation 13:11-18, will make an image of the first beast, "whose fatal wound was healed" (verse 12). It would be strange for the second beast to construct an image of an *empire* that had died and come back to life. It makes more sense, then, to understand the beast as a person.

Second, would the revival of the Roman Empire really cause the entire world to be awestruck, as is described in Revelation 13:3? This verse says that after the beast is slain and comes back to life, "the whole earth" will be "amazed" and follow after the beast. This is *the* event that propels the beast to great popularity and causes all the world to fall at his feet. Such a response would be much more likely if this were referring to a man rather than an empire. A revival of the Roman Empire would hardly leave the world dumbstruck and cause everyone to be amazed and follow the empire. But if a great world leader were assassinated with a fatal head wound and then came back to life a few days later, then we would expect such an overwhelming response.

Bible commentator John Phillips captures the meaning well when he says,

> With this master stroke of miracle, the devil brings the world to the feet of the messiah…It is this miracle of his resurrection that is given as the reason for the popularity of the Beast. No doubt the whole thing will be stage-managed by Satan and the false prophet to make the greatest possible impact upon men. Their propaganda

machine will see to it that the miracle is magnified and elaborated to the fullest extent.[4]

A third reason for believing Revelation 13:3-4 and 17:8 apply to a man rather than the revived empire is that, as Warren Wiersbe says, "it would be difficult to understand how a kingdom could be slain by a sword. It is best, I think, to apply this prophecy to individual persons."[5] I agree. The leader of the reunited Roman Empire is the primary figure in view in Revelation 13:1-10. But that brings us to the next question.

Parody or Reality?

The other two views of this death and resurrection are that it refers to an individual. That, of course, brings us to a question many Christians ask: Is this resurrection of the beast during the Tribulation for real, or is it just a cheap trick? Is it authentic or just a counterfeit?

Many reputable and solid Bible commentators and prophecy teachers hold to the view that because Satan does not have the power to give life, this will only *appear* to be a real death and resurrection. They say the Antichrist will not really die. For example, J. Vernon McGee said,

> Only Christ can raise the dead—both saved and lost. Satan has no power to raise the dead. He is not a life-giver. He is a devil, a destroyer, a death-dealer…I believe the beast is a man who will exhibit a counterfeit and imitation resurrection. This will be the great delusion, the big lie of the Great Tribulation Period…They will not accept the resurrection of Christ, but they sure are going to fake the resurrection of the Antichrist…Nobody can duplicate the resurrection of Christ; they might imitate it, but

they cannot duplicate it. Yet Antichrist is going to imitate it in a way that will fool the world—it is the big lie. Believers say, "Christ is risen!" The boast of unbelievers in that day will be: "So is Antichrist!" The Roman Empire will spring back into existence under the cruel hand of a man who faked a resurrection, and a gullible world who rejected Christ will finally be taken in by this forgery.[6]

While I wholeheartedly agree with those who say that only God has the power to resurrect the dead, I (and some other Bible teachers and commentators) believe the Antichrist will parody Christ so completely that he will actually die and come back to life. Let me explain what leads me to this conclusion.

First, I believe that the signs, wonders, and miracles done through satanic agency are indeed miraculous. Jesus (in Matthew 24:4-5,11,24), Paul (in 2 Thessalonians 2:9), and John (in Revelation 13:13-15; 16:13-14; 19:20) all describe the miraculous works accomplished through Satan's oversight using the very same language used to describe the miracles performed by Jesus Himself. It appears that during the Tribulation, a time during which the restrainer will be removed, unparalleled satanic power will be unleashed. God the Holy Spirit is now restraining the Antichrist from certain activity during the current era (2 Thessalonians 2:6-7). But once the Holy Spirit steps aside, the world will see a dramatic increase in the amount and extent of satanic activity: "the one whose coming is in accord with the activity of Satan, with all power and signs and false wonders" (2 Thessalonians 2:9).

Paul specifically said that "God will send upon them a deluding influence" (2 Thessalonians 2:11). That is, God will "send" this activity upon the people of the world. His purpose is "so that they will believe what is false, in order that they all may be judged who did not believe the truth, but took pleasure in wickedness" (2 Thessalonians 2:11-12).

Now, let's consider a few reasons why it appears that the beast of Revelation will rise from the dead and perform genuine miracles during the Tribulation.

Signs, Wonders, and Miracles

In the New Testament, the language primarily used to describe the miracles of Christ and the apostles are the terms "signs," "wonders," and "miracles." The Greek word for "sign" is *semeion* and means "sign" or "distinguishing mark" by which something is known. It is used of miracles by Christ and the apostles in many passages (Matthew 12:38; 16:1,4; Mark 8:11,12; 16:17,20; Luke 11:16,29; 23:8; John 2:11,18,23; 3:2; 4:48,54; 6:2,14,26,30; 7:31; 9:16; Acts 2:22,43; 4:16,30; 5:12; 6:8; 7:36; 14:3; 15:12; Romans 15:19; 1 Corinthians 1:22; 2 Corinthians 12:12; Hebrews 2:4).[7] This is the most common word used to describe the miraculous works of Christ and His apostles.

Miracles in the New Testament are also referred to by the Greek word *teras,* which is translated into English as "a wonder, marvel."[8] The noun "wonder" occurs 16 times in the New Testament and is always coupled with the word "sign" (Matthew 24:24; Mark 13:22; John 4:48; Acts 2:19,22,43; 4:30; 5:12; 6:8; 7:36; 14:3; 15:12; Romans 15:19; 2 Corinthians 12:12; 2 Thessalonians 2:9; Hebrews 2:4). All those passages except 2 Thessalonians 2:9 describe the miracles done by Christ and the apostles and note "something so strange as to cause it to be 'watched' or 'observed.'"[9]

The remaining Greek words used to speak of miracles are *dunamis* and *energeia,* which are usually translated as "miracle" and "working." "Both point more to the supernatural source

rather than to what is produced,"[10] concludes Harris. Other than
2 Thessalonians 2:9, these words always refer to "the workings of
God."[11] Philip Edgcumbe Hughes ties it all together with the following statement:

> It is best to take signs, wonders, and miracles as belonging
> together rather than as indicating three different forms
> of manifestation…Thus a sign, which is the word con-
> sistently used in the Fourth Gospel for the miraculous
> works of Christ, indicates that the event is not an empty
> ostentation of power, but is significant in that, sign-wise,
> it points beyond itself to the reality of the mighty hand of
> God in operation. A wonder is an event which because
> of its superhuman character, excites awe and amazement
> on the part of the beholder. A miracle (or literally power)
> emphasizes the dynamic character of the event, with par-
> ticular regard to its outcome or effect.[12]

Amazingly, the words just noted to describe the miraculous
work of Christ and the apostles are also the terms used to describe
"the miracles performed in the Tribulation by those in allegiance
with Satan."[13] The word "signs" is used of satanic miracles in the
Tribulation (Revelation 13:13-14; 16:14), "and the same combina-
tion of words is used: great signs and wonders (Matt. 24:24: Mark
13:22), all power and signs and wonder (2 Thessalonians 2:9)."[14]
Of special note is 2 Thessalonians 2:9, which says of the man of
lawlessness that he is "the one whose coming is in accord with the
activity of Satan, with all power and signs and false wonders." It
sounds like the Bible is telling us that these are miracles similar to
the ones done by our Lord. "The word *pseudos* ('false') has to do
with the results of the miracles, not with their lack of genuineness
or supernatural origin."[15] The language used by the inspired New

Testament writers will not allow for a meaning that these satanic works arc just slcight-of-hand magic tricks, as wc will soon scc.

> Then that lawless one will be revealed whom the Lord will slay with the breath of His mouth and bring to an end by the appearance of His coming; that is, the one whose coming is in accord with the activity of Satan, with all power and signs and false wonders, and with all the deception of wickedness for those who perish, because they did not receive the love of the truth so as to be saved. For this reason God will send upon them a deluding influence so that they will believe what is false, in order that they all may be judged who did not believe the truth, but took pleasure in wickedness (2 Thessalonians 2:8-12).

So the Bible passages that speak of satanic miracles preformed through the Antichrist and the false prophet use the exact same language that was used of Christ's miracles at His first advent. This fact supports the notion that the Tribulation will be a unique time in history during which God permits Satan to do miracles so he can deceive those who reject Christ's offer of salvation.

Identical Language

Revelation 13:3 tells us the beast will have a "fatal wound" that is "healed." The chapter also says that the false prophet "makes the earth and those who dwell in it to worship the first beast, whose fatal wound was healed" (13:12); "performs great signs, so that he even makes fire come down out of heaven to the earth in the presence of men" (13:13); "he deceives those who dwell on the earth because of the signs which it was given him to perform in the presence of the beast, telling those who dwell on the earth...to make an image to the beast who had the wound of the sword and has come to life" (13:14); and "it was given to him to give breath to the image of the beast, that the image of the beast would even speak" (13:15). If Satan will be given the power to give life to a dead idol, as Revelation 13:15 states, then why would it not also be possible for him (with God's permission) to resurrect a man from the dead? [16]

As Gregory Harris observes, "In support of the view that this wound was fatal is the fact that identical language is used of Christ's death and resurrection."[17] Revelation 5:6 describes the Lamb as if slain [*hos esphagmenen*], the same words used of the wound received by the beast (*hos esphagmenen*) in Revelation 13:3. Because of this close similarity Ryrie concludes, "If Christ died actually, then it appears that this ruler will also actually die. But his wound would be healed, which can only mean restoration to life…He apparently dies, descends to the abyss and returns to life."[18]

Furthermore, "the word referring to the beast's return to life is similar to the word used of Christ's return to life. Jesus is the One 'who was dead and has come to life [*ezesen*]' (Revelation 2:8). And the beast will be the one 'who had the wound of the sword and has come to life [*ezesen*]' (13:14)."[19] Comparing the statements about Christ's death in Revelation 5:6 and the death of the beast in Revelation 13, J.B. Smith says, "Since the words in the former instance signify the death of Christ by violence, so truly will the final Roman emperor meet a violent death. In each instance the marks or insignia of a violent death are apparent."[20]

In support of this understanding is the fact that Revelation 17:8,11 refers to the beast which "was and is not." Gregory Harris notes, "This may well refer to the wounding of the Antichrist in 13:3, 12, and 14. The words 'is not' refer to the physical death of the beast, followed by his ascent from the abyss (17:8), which refers to his return to life (13:14) and is the same as his reappearance as the eighth king of 17:11."[21] As John Phillips notes, "The Beast has two comings. He appears first as the 'beast…out of the sea' (13:1), and later, after his assassination, as the 'beast…out of the abyss' (17:8)."[22]

Second Thessalonians 2:11-12 says, "For this reason God will send upon them a deluding influence so that they will believe what is false, in order that they all may be judged who did not believe the truth, but took pleasure in wickedness." God is the one who will enable Satan and his followers to do miracles similar to the genuine miracles done by Jesus and the disciples. Harris tells us,

> The possibility of the beast's return to life (with either God's sovereign permission or His active working) should not be readily ruled out. In other words it is not impossible that the Antichrist should return to life because of the unique status of the Tribulation and the increased capacity of satanic power during that time, as well as God's broadening the parameters of what He will either permit or accomplish directly.[23]

For these reasons, I believe the Antichrist will truly die and come back to life—in a striking parody of the death and resurrection of Jesus Christ. This stunning event will happen at the midpoint of the seven-year Tribulation and will coincide with Satan being cast out of heaven and having but a short time to do his evil work (Revelation 12:12). Realizing that time is running out, Satan will duplicate the resurrection of Christ and indwell the Antichrist. This will be part of the dramatic deception that God will allow during that special season of time at the end of the age. From that point onward, having come back from perdition and being indwelt by Satan, Antichrist will have the power to perform all kinds of signs, wonders, and miracles and will unleash his final great work of deception.

J.B. Smith describes the impact this astonishing event will have on the world in the end times: "Just as the early spread and the perpetuity of the Christian faith are grounded upon the resurrection of Christ, so the all but universal worship and homage accorded the beast in the last half of the tribulation period can only be accounted for by the resurrection of the fallen emperor of Rome."[24]

Who is the false prophet, and what is his relationship to the Antichrist?

According to Revelation 13:11-18, the Antichrist will not rise to power alone. He will be catapulted to power and enjoy unparalleled success as a result of the worldwide deception promoted by a man Scripture calls "the false prophet" (Revelation 16:13). His ability to perform stunning miracles, signs, and wonders will enable him to convince the world that the Antichrist is the leader they've been looking for—the man with a plan, the man who can solve the world's problems.

There have always been false prophets and teachers. One of Satan's chief methods of operation is to counterfeit and corrupt the true message of God through false messengers. And he will do this all the more during the end times. The Bible says that in the last days of planet Earth there will come many false prophets who will perform great signs and wonders and spew out deceiving lies (Matthew 24:24). In this mass of deception, one false prophet will rise high above all the rest in his ability to capture the world's attention. He is called "the false prophet" three times in Revelation (16:13; 19:20; 20:10), and he is also known as "another beast," or the second beast, in Revelation 13:11-18.

While a great deal has been written about the Antichrist,

comparatively little has been written about the false prophet. Yet he is a central figure in the coming events of the Tribulation. He is the final person in the unholy trinity of the end times (see Revelation 16:13; 19:20–20:2; 20:10). As Donald Grey Barnhouse said,

> The devil is making his last and greatest effort, a furious effort, to gain power and establish his kingdom upon the earth. He knows nothing better than to imitate God. Since God has succeeded by means of an incarnation and then by means of the work of the Holy Spirit, the devil will work by means of an incarnation in Antichrist and by the unholy spirit.[25]

In hell's trinity, Satan is a counterfeit Father (the anti-Father), the Antichrist is a counterfeit Son (the anti-Christ), and the false prophet is the satanic counterfeit of the Holy Spirit (the anti-Spirit). This is the infernal trinity.

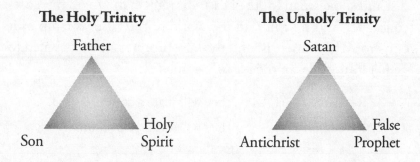

The Holy Trinity — Father, Son, Holy Spirit

The Unholy Trinity — Satan, Antichrist, False Prophet

Just as a key ministry of the Holy Spirit is to glorify Christ and lead people to trust and worship Him, a key ministry of the false prophet will be to glorify the Antichrist and lead people to trust and worship him. Here are five key ways the false prophet will counterfeit the ministry of the Holy Spirit:

Holy Spirit	False Prophet
Points men to Christ	Points men to Antichrist
Instrument of divine revelation	Instrument of satanic revelation
Seals believers to God	Marks unbelievers with the number of Antichrist
Builds the body of Christ	Builds the empire of Antichrist
Enlightens men with the truth	Deceives men by miracles

The Antichrist, or the first beast of Revelation 13, will primarily be a military and political figure, whereas the second beast will primarily be a religious figure. He will be a kind of "satanic John the Baptist" who prepares the way for the coming of the Antichrist. The false prophet will be the chief propagandist and spokesman for the beast, his right-hand man, his closest colleague. And he will lead the world in the false worship of its emperor. The Antichrist and the false prophet are mentioned together four places in the New Testament:

1. Revelation 13:1-18   They will share a common goal.

2. Revelation 16:13   They will share a common agenda for the world.

3. Revelation 19:20   They will share a common sentence.

4. Revelation 20:10   They will share a common destiny.

Thomas Ice and Timothy Demy note this close connection: "The Antichrist and the False Prophet are two separate individuals who will work toward a common, deceptive goal. Their roles and relationships will be that which was common in the ancient world between a ruler (Antichrist) and the high priest (False Prophet) of the national religion."[26]

Jew or Gentile?

Bible scholars are divided over the ethnic identity of the false prophet. Some believe he will be a Jew, while others maintain he will be a Gentile. Those who believe he will be of Jewish ancestry point to Revelation 13:11: "I saw another beast coming up out of the earth; and he had two horns like a lamb and he spoke as a dragon." Revelation 13:1 says that the first beast, the political ruler, will come up "out of the sea." As was noted earlier, in Revelation, the sea is symbolic of the Gentile nations (Revelation 17:15). But in Revelation 13:11, many prophecy teachers take the word "earth" to mean "land" or to be a reference to the land of Israel. Thus they conclude the second beast must be a Jew. While it's certainly possible that "earth" refers to Israel, it seems better to see the word "earth" as a contrast to heaven. Whatever the case, however, the Bible is inconclusive on this matter. It just doesn't tell us enough to know the answer for certain. But because the second beast works so closely with the Antichrist, who appears from the biblical record to be a Gentile, it make sense that the false prophet will also be a Gentile.

Work of the False Prophet

There are three key elements of the false prophet's work as described by Revelation 13:11-18: his deceptive appearance, his devilish authority, and his deadly activity.

His Deceptive Appearance (Revelation 13:11)

"Then I saw another beast coming up out of the earth; and he had two horns like a lamb and he spoke as a dragon." This is total deception! Here is a man who is described as a wild beast, a lamb, and dragon.

He has the nature of a wild beast.	He is hostile to God's flock and ravages God's people.
He has the appearance of a lamb.	He looks gentle, tender, mild, and harmless.
He has the voice of a dragon.	He is the voice of hell itself belching forth the fiery lies of Satan. When he speaks, he serves as Satan's mouthpiece.

John Phillips summarizes the deceptive appearance and deadly approach of the false prophet:

> The role of the false prophet will be to make the new religion appealing and palatable to men. No doubt it will combine all the features of the religious systems of men, will appeal to man's total personality, and will take full advantage of his carnal appetite. The dynamic appeal of the false prophet will lie in his skill in combining political expediency with religious passion, self-interest with benevolent philanthropy, lofty sentiment with blatant sophistry, moral platitude with unbridled self-indulgence. His arguments will be subtle, convincing, and appealing. His oratory will be hypnotic, for he will be able to move the masses to tears or whip them into a frenzy. He will control the communication media of the world and will skillfully organize mass publicity to promote his ends. He will be the master of every promotional device and public relations gimmick. He will manage the truth with guile beyond words, bending it,

twisting it, and distorting it. Public opinion will be his to command. He will mold world thought and shape human opinion like so much potter's clay. His deadly appeal will lie in the fact that what he says will sound so right, so sensible, so exactly what unregenerate men have always wanted to hear.[27]

His Devilish Authority (Revelation 13:12)

Revelation 13:12 says the second beast "exercises all the authority of the first beast in his presence. And he makes the earth and those who dwell in it to worship the first beast, whose fatal wound was healed." That is, the false prophet will have great authority delegated to him by the Antichrist. His mission will be to use every means given to him by the Antichrist to cause everyone on earth to worship the beast. He will carry out the plans and wishes of the Antichrist and lead the worldwide cult of Antichrist worship. He will also be empowered by the same source as the first beast—Satan himself. As happened with Joseph Goebbels and Hitler, he will be inspired by the same authority and share the same diabolical agenda as the Antichrist.

His Deadly Activity (Revelation 13:13-18)

Seven deadly activities of the false prophet are delineated in Revelation 13:13-18. These activities reveal how he will use his influence and experience during the days of the Great Tribulation

1. He will come up out of the earth (13:11)

As already noted, some students of Bible prophecy have taken this to mean that the false prophet will be a Jew. The first beast or Antichrist will come up out of the sea, which may indicate he is a Gentile. The second beast, or the false prophet, will come up out of the earth or land, which some believe could refer to Israel.

However it is better to see the false prophet as a Gentile. Keep in mind that the second beast will help the first beast persecute the Jewish people, so it is doubtful he will be of Jewish descent. The fact he is said to come up out of the earth is probably meant to contrast him in some way with the Holy Spirit, who comes down from heaven. The false prophet will be someone "earthly" in the fullest sense of the word. The earth will be his domain and his sole focus.

2. He will bring down fire from heaven and perform other miracles (13:13-14)

The false prophet will mimic the miracles of the two witnesses (in Revelation 11:4-6), just as the ancient Egyptian magicians counterfeited the miracles of Moses (Exodus 7:11-13,22; 8:7). Thomas Ice and Tim Demy provide a practical word of caution in response to alleged miracles we might hear about in our day: "Even though this is yet a future event, the lesson to be learned for our own day is that one must exercise discernment, especially in the area of religion—even when miracles appear to vindicate the messenger."[28]

3. He will erect an image to the Antichrist for all the world to worship (13:14)

As we have already seen, this image or abomination of desolation will undoubtedly be placed in the temple in Jerusalem (Matthew 24:15). As was the case with the image of Nebuchadnezzar on the plain of Dura (Daniel 3), all will have to bow to this image or die.

4. He will raise the Antichrist from the dead (13:14)

While this is not stated explicitly in the text, it is strongly implied. The death and resurrection of the Antichrist is mentioned three times in Revelation 13 (verses 3,12,14) and also in Revelation

17:8. Because the false prophet is a miracle worker who will deceive the world, it is probable that Satan will use the false prophet as his human instrument to raise the Antichrist back to life.

5. He will give life to the image of the beast (13:15)

The image that is erected in the beast's honor won't be like any other image ever created. Like something out of a science fiction or horror film, it will be animated. It will speak and breathe. Satan's deception will reach its zenith under the final world ruler and his passionate promoter.

6. He will control world commerce on behalf of the beast, forcing everyone to take the mark of the beast (13:16)

The crowning achievement of the second beast will be the implementation of a global registration of all people so that they are set up to take the mark of the beast. He will use total control of the economy to secure the rule of the first beast, the Antichrist. No one will be able to buy or sell without pledging allegiance to the beast, receiving his mark, and submitting to the global registration system. His economic program is set forth in Revelation 13:16-17:

> He causes all, the small and the great, and the rich and the poor, and the free men and the slaves, to be given a mark on their right hand or on their forehead, and he provides that no one will be able to buy or to sell, except the one who has the mark, either the name of the beast or the number of his name.

Notice the universal scope of this control. It will extend to "all." The false prophet will exercise iron-fisted control over the basic fundamentals of the world economy—supply (no one will be able to sell) and demand (no one will be able to buy). No one will be able to go to the mall, eat at a restaurant, fill their gas tank, pay their utility bills, buy groceries, pay to get their lawn mowed, or make a mortgage payment without the mark of the beast.

Ten Identifying Features of the False Prophet

1. Rises out of the earth (13:11)
2. Controls religious affairs (13:11)
3. Motivated by Satan (13:11)
4. Promotes worship of the first beast (13:12)
5. Perform signs and miracles (13:13)
6. Deceives the whole world (13:14)
7. Empowers the image of the beast (13:15)
8. Kills all who refuse to worship the image (13:15)
9. Controls all commerce (13:17)
10. Controls the mark of the beast (13:17-18)

What is the "abomination of desolation" that the Antichrist will introduce?

For at least a portion of the first half of the Tribulation, the Jewish people, under their covenant with the Antichrist, will have a rebuilt Temple and will be able to offer sacrifices, according to Daniel 9:27. However, at the midpoint of the seven-year Tribulation, that will all change. Daniel 9:27 says, "In the middle of the week he will put a stop to sacrifice and grain offering; and on the wing of abominations will come one who makes desolate, even until a complete destruction, one that is decreed, is poured out on the one who makes desolate." At this point, the Antichrist will break his covenant with Israel and commit an act that is most often called "the abomination of desolation."

What Scripture Says

This monumental end-time act of sacrilege is mentioned specifically by name several times in Scripture:

Daniel 9:27

He will make a firm covenant with the many for one week, but in the middle of the week he will put a stop to sacrifice and grain offering; and on the wing of abominations will come one who makes desolate, even until a complete destruction, one that is decreed, is poured out on the one who makes desolate.

Daniel 12:11

From the time that the regular sacrifice is abolished and the abomination of desolation is set up, there will be 1,290 days.

Matthew 24:15-16

When you see the abomination of desolation which was spoken of through Daniel the prophet, standing in the holy place...then those who are in Judea must flee to the mountains.

Mark 13:14

When you see the abomination of desolation standing where it should not be (let the reader understand), then those who are in Judea must flee to the mountains.

Those passages make it abundantly clear that the Jewish people will rebuild the Temple in Jerusalem sometime before the midpoint of the Tribulation.

Now, what exactly is the abomination of desolation? First, we need to know that word "abomination" refers to an idol or image. Second, the first reference to the abomination of desolation—in Daniel 9:27—links it with Antichrist's breaking of the covenant with Israel. There, we read that the Antichrist "will put a stop to sacrifice and grain offering" at the Temple. The phrase "on the wing of abominations" refers to the pinnacle of the Temple, emphasizing the idea of an overspreading influence. In other words, what the Antichrist does at the Temple will spread to other places.[29] The abomination of desolation, then, is an idol or image that desolates the Temple and spreads out from there to the world.

A Repeat Performance

The abomination that the Antichrist will perpetrate during the Tribulation will be a repeat of what the Seleucid (Syrian) king Antiochus IV (Epiphanes) did in 167 BC in the Jewish Temple. He invaded the city of Jerusalem and his soldiers pillaged the Temple, defiled it by offering an unclean animal (pig) on the Temple altar. They stopped the Jewish sacrifices and instituted pagan worship by erecting a statue of Zeus Olympias in the Holy of Holies. Coincidentally, the face on the statue of Zeus "just happened" to look like the face of Antiochus. This event is described in the non-canonical books of 1 Maccabees 1:10-63 and 2 Maccabees 5:1ff.

Amazingly, Antiochus's action was predicted by the prophet Daniel about 400 years before it occurred:

> It even magnified itself to be equal with the Commander
> of the host; and it removed the regular sacrifice from
> Him, and the place of His sanctuary was thrown down.

And on account of transgression the host will be given over to the horn along with the regular sacrifice; and it will fling truth to the ground and perform its will and prosper. Then I heard a holy one speaking, and another holy one said to that particular one who was speaking, "How long will the vision about the regular sacrifice apply, while the transgression causes horror, so as to allow both the holy place and the host to be trampled?" He said to me, "For 2,300 evenings and mornings; then the holy place will be properly restored" (Daniel 8:11-14).

In his place a despicable person will arise, on whom the honor of kingship has not been conferred, but he will come in a time of tranquility and seize the kingdom by intrigue... Forces from him will arise, desecrate the sanctuary fortress, and do away with the regular sacrifice. And they will set up the abomination of desolation (Daniel 11:21,31).

Antiochus committed other atrocities. He burned copies of the Torah, forced Jewish people to consume pork in violation of the Mosaic law, and mandated pagan sacrifices. On December 25, 164 BC, the Jewish leader Judas Maccabeus restored the Jewish ritual by cleansing and rededicating the Temple. This is what brought about the Jewish Festival of Lights, or Hanukkah. With all of that in mind, let's look now at what Scripture says about the future abomination of desolation committed by the Antichrist.

Two Future Phases of the Abomination

It appears from Scripture that there are two main elements or phases involved in the abomination of desolation that takes place during the end times.[30] The initial phase is described for us in 2 Thessalonians 2:3-4:

Let no one in any way deceive you, for it will not come unless the apostasy comes first, and the man of lawlessness is revealed, the son of destruction, who opposes and exalts himself above every so-called god or object of worship, so that he takes his seat in the temple of God, displaying himself as being God.

When the Antichrist first takes over Jerusalem, he will sit in the very Holy of Holies in the Temple and declare to the world that he is God. In doing this he will establish the false religion he desires to impose upon the entire world.

The second phase regarding the abomination of desolation is set forth in Revelation 13:11-15:

I saw another beast coming up out of the earth; and he had two horns like a lamb and he spoke as a dragon. He exercises all the authority of the first beast in his presence. And he makes the earth and those who dwell in it to worship the first beast, whose fatal wound was healed. And he performs great signs, so that he even makes fire come down out of heaven to the earth in the presence of men. And he deceives those who dwell on the earth because of the signs which it was given him to perform in the presence of the beast, telling those who dwell on the earth to make an image to the beast who had the wound of the sword and has come to life. And there was given to him to give breath to the image of the beast, so that the image of the beast would even speak and cause as many as do not worship the image of the beast to be killed.

The Antichrist will not be able to sit in the Temple 24/7 to receive worship, so he will have an image or idol of his likeness constructed to sit in the Temple in his place. That an idol will be involved is clear from the meaning of the word "abomination" ("idol") as well as the actions of Antiochus in setting up the image. Warren Wiersbe explains, "What is the abomination of desolation? It is the image of 'the beast,' set up in the temple in Israel in Jerusalem. An idol is bad enough; but setting it up in the temple is the height of all blasphemy. Since Satan could not command worship in heaven, he will go to the next best place—the Jewish temple in the Holy City."[31]

The Antichrist's right-hand man, the false prophet, whom we met in the previous chapter, will be given the authority to do great signs and wonders and will deceive people into worshiping the beast. His greatest deception will be the construction of an image or likeness of the Antichrist and bringing it to life.

This image, as was the case with the abomination committed by Antiochus, will be placed in the Holy of Holies in the rebuilt Temple in Jerusalem. Jerusalem will serve as the Antichrist's religious world capital, and the Temple will serve as the center of worship with the living image standing in its inner precinct. All the earth will be required to worship the beast's image or face death.

The two phases of the abomination of desolation, therefore, will be (1) the Antichrist's entrance into the Holy of Holies and his declaration that he is God, (2) followed by the setting up of his image in that same place. This condition will persist for the final 1260 days or three-and-a-half years of the Tribulation.[32]

Why will the Antichrist persecute the Jewish people?

One of the paramount pursuits of the coming Antichrist, according to Scripture, will be a merciless persecution of the Jewish people. Antichrist will be the final, brutal anti-Semite, hounding the Jews until the very end. This pursuit is repeatedly emphasized in Scripture. We find it first in Daniel 7:

> I desired to know the exact meaning of the fourth beast, which was different from all the others, exceedingly dreadful, with its teeth of iron and its claws of bronze, and which devoured, crushed and trampled down the remainder with its feet, and the meaning of the ten horns that were on its head and the other horn which came up, and before which three of them fell, namely, that horn which had eyes and a mouth uttering great boasts and which was larger in appearance than its associates. I kept looking, and that horn was waging war with the saints and overpowering them until the Ancient of Days came and judgment was passed in favor of the saints of the Highest One, and the time arrived when the saints took possession of the kingdom...He will speak out against the Most High and wear down the saints of the Highest One, and he will intend to make alterations in times and in law; and they will be given into his hand for a time, times, and half a time (verses 19-22,25).

The context of Daniel 7 tells us the "saints" that the little horn or Antichrist is oppressing are the Jewish people. Daniel 9:27 tells of Antichrist's seven-year covenant of peace with Israel at the beginning of the Tribulation, as well as his great double-cross at the midpoint of the seven years and his turning against the Jews as a ferocious desolator:

> He will make a firm covenant with the many for one week [one week of years, or seven years], but in the middle of the week he will put a stop to sacrifice and grain offering; and on the wing of abominations will come one who makes

desolate, even until a complete destruction, one that is decreed, is poured out on the one who makes desolate.

Jesus spoke of this coming time of worldwide persecution of the Jews in conjunction with the breaking of the seven-year covenant and the abomination of desolation that will be set up in Jerusalem by the Antichrist:

> When you see the ABOMINATION OF DESOLATION which was spoken of through Daniel the prophet, standing in the holy place (let the reader understand), then those who are in Judea must flee to the mountains. Whoever is on the housetop must not go down to get the things out that are in his house. Whoever is in the field must not turn back to get his cloak. But woe to those who are pregnant and to those who are nursing babies in those days! But pray that your flight will not be in the winter, or on a Sabbath. For then there will be a great tribulation, such as has not occurred since the beginning of the world until now, nor ever will. Unless those days had been cut short, no life would have been saved; but for the sake of the elect those days will be cut short (Matthew 24:15-22).

Jesus warns the Jews living at that time to flee and get out of Israel as quickly as possible.

Another key passage of Scripture that highlights the end-time pogrom against the Jews is Revelation 12. In this highly symbolic chapter Satan is pictured as a "great red dragon" (verse 3) and the nation of Israel is symbolized by "a woman clothed with the sun, and the moon under her feet, and on her head a crown of twelve stars; and she was with child; and she cried out, being in labor and in pain to give birth" (verses 1-2). We know this woman is Israel because the imagery in Revelation 12:1 is a clear allusion to

Genesis 37:9, which is the only place in the Bible where we find all these same symbols clustered together in one place. Genesis 37:9 records a dream Joseph had, a dream in which his father, mother, and 11 brothers—represented by the sun, moon, and 11 starts—bowed down before him. The woman in Revelation 12 represents the people of Israel, all of whom are descendants of Jacob. Joseph would be the twelfth star. This imagery encompasses the entire nation. Also, in Revelation 12:2, the woman is said to be with child, and the child is clearly Jesus. According to Isaiah 9:6, it was the Jewish nation that would give birth to the Messiah: "For a child will be born to us, a son will be given to us."

Employing this imagery, Revelation 12 goes on to graphically depict the original fall of Satan and the one-third of the angels who joined his ill-fated rebellion, and Satan's murderous attempts to destroy the baby Jesus through King Herod. Satan wanted to keep Jesus from fulfilling His saving work on the cross. Satan tried many times in the Old Testament to get rid of the Jewish people because he wanted to keep the promised Messiah from coming. Think of Pharaoh's order to kill the male Israelite babies, Haman's edict to slaughter the Jews (in the book of Esther), and the massacres under Antiochus Epiphanes during the intertestamental period.

Someone has pointed out that every time someone tries to wipe out the Jews they get a holiday in observance of the occasion. With Pharaoh they got Passover, with Haman they got the Feast of Purim, and with Antiochus Epiphanes they got Hanukkah or the Feast of Lights. One could even say that as a result of the holocaust under Hitler, the Jews got May 14, 1948, the day on which the modern state of Israel was born. God has made eternal, unconditional covenants with Israel—He has promised the land in the Abrahamic Covenant (Genesis 15:17-21), the kingdom in the Davidic Covenant (2 Samuel 7:12-16), and spiritual restoration in the New Covenant (Jeremiah 31:31-34). All these covenants were made with Israel and must be fulfilled with Israel.

As vicious as the past attacks on the Jewish people have been, the culmination of the satanic war against Israel is slated on God's calendar for the end times, primarily during the final three-and-a-half years of the Tribulation. Satan will organize an all-out, worldwide anti-Semitic campaign to try to eliminate all the Jewish people once and for all.

> Then the woman fled into the wilderness where she had a place prepared by God, so that there she would be nourished for one thousand two hundred and sixty days... And when the dragon saw that he was thrown down to the earth, he persecuted the woman who gave birth to the male child. But the two wings of the great eagle were given to the woman, so that she could fly into the wilderness to her place, where she was nourished for a time and times and half a time, from the presence of the serpent. And the serpent poured water like a river out of his mouth after the woman, so that he might cause her to be swept away with the flood. But the earth helped the woman, and the earth opened its mouth and drank up the river which the dragon poured out of his mouth. So the dragon was enraged with the woman, and went off to make war with the rest of her children, who keep the commandments of God and hold to the testimony of Jesus (Revelation 12:6,13-17).

There are many aspects of this passage that we don't have the space to consider at this time, but the main point is that in the end times Satan and his demonic host will launch the final, desperate phase of the war of the ages in a feverish attempt to keep God from fulfilling His good promises to the Jewish people. In response, the Jews will escape to the desert, possibly the city of Petra, south of the Dead Sea, and the swiftness of their flight is symbolized by eagle's wings (Revelation 12:14). Some have speculated that the mention of eagle's wings is a reference to the U.S. Air Force carrying out an emergency airlift of the Jews, but this kind of conjecture is unwarranted. Identical imagery is found in Exodus 19:4 and Deuteronomy 32:11 in relation to God's supernatural deliverance of the Jewish people from Egypt during the exodus.

Now, you might be wondering, *What does all this have to do with the Antichrist and the Jews?* Here's the important connection: The Antichrist is the human instrument that Satan will use to wage his war against the Jews. After Revelation 12 describes this final satanic onslaught against Israel, the next chapter continues the vision of the woman and the dragon and opens with these chilling words: "The dragon stood on the sand of the seashore. Then I saw a beast coming up out of the sea, having ten horns and seven heads, and on his horns were ten diadems, and on his heads were blasphemous names" (Revelation 13:1). This means that Satan, in his attack on the Jews, will call the beast out of the sea, who is the final Antichrist, to come help him in this pursuit. Satan will stand on the seashore and beckon the beast to come and be the instrument through which this persecution will be unleashed. Antichrist will be the tool, the channel, the human catalyst that Satan will fill and empower to carry out his "final solution" in waging war against the Jewish people.

Arthur E. Bloomfield, in his book *How to Recognize the Antichrist*, aptly describes the Antichrist's attitude toward the Jews:

> Antichrist's attitude toward the Jews will probably be

evident from the start. It will be the same as Hitler's was, except that the Antichrist will attempt to destroy *all* the Jews on the face of the earth. It must be remembered that Antichrist is a protégé of Satan and will carry out Satan's program. Satan's attempt to destroy the Jews is of long standing. A number of times in history the Jews have narrowly escaped; in fact, the history of Israel is a history of narrow escapes...The history of the Jews is a history of expulsion from one country to another. Whenever Satan gets the upper hand, the Jews are in trouble.[33]

Bloomfield then presents the nefarious reason behind this age-long satanic plot.

God's whole future program revolves around Israel... God's entire kingdom program revolves around Israel. When Christ comes again, according to the prophet Zechariah, His feet shall stand upon the Mount of Olives that is before Jerusalem. The Jews will be the nucleus of the new kingdom. If Satan is to win this war and retain control of the earth, he must of necessity destroy all the Jews. That would prevent the establishing of the kingdom of God in the world. This is the basic program of Satan. His first attempt, when he gets control of the earth, will be to destroy all Jews. This will provoke the greatest crisis in the history of Israel. This particular feature of the character and work of the Antichrist will be so prominent that it will be a positive mark of identification.[34]

Israel will be the final target of Satan and his man, the Antichrist. Revelation 16:13-16 describes the place where troops from all over the world will mobilize under Antichrist's command in their final, futile attempt to destroy Israel.

I saw coming out of the mouth of the dragon and out of the mouth of the beast and out of the mouth of the false prophet, three unclean spirits like frogs; for they are spirits of demons, performing signs, which go out to the kings of the whole world, to gather them together for the war of the great day of God, the Almighty. ("Behold, I am coming like a thief. Blessed is the one who stays awake and keeps his clothes, so that he will not walk about naked and men will not see his shame.") And they gathered them together to the place which in Hebrew is called Har-Magedon.

Har-Magedon, or Armageddon, which is in the northern part of Israel, will serve as a kind of staging ground or mobilization center for the armies of the world. The battle will be over the city of Jerusalem, as Zechariah describes: "Behold, I am going to make Jerusalem a cup that causes reeling to all the peoples around; and when the siege is against Jerusalem, it will also be against Judah. It will come about in that day that I will make Jerusalem a heavy stone for all the peoples; all who lift it will be severely injured. And all the nations of the earth will be gathered against it" (Zechariah 12:2-3; cf. Joel 3:2,12). The glorious second coming of Jesus to earth will climax the Campaign of Armageddon as Jesus splits the sky and comes to destroy the Antichrist and the false prophet and cast them alive into the Lake of Fire (Revelation 19:20-21).

While the events we see taking place in the world today are not the fulfillment of these prophecies in Daniel and Revelation, we must acknowledge that the world is once again quickly turning against the nation of Israel. This tiny nation that is about the size of New Jersey is in the headlines every day. The people of Israel are demonized and castigated by the world as they try to survive in the midst of a sea of enemies. The world clamors for peace in the Middle East, and Israel is in the eye of the storm. One wonders how much longer the Jewish people can hang on before the lid blows off. Yet the Bible tells us that after the rapture of the church and the dramatic weakening of America as a result, Israel will turn to the Antichrist to protect her against the adversaries who surround her. He will feign a concern for Israel at the beginning and forge a peace agreement, but will break his treaty at its midpoint and serve as an instrument of Satan's final attempt to wipe out the Jews and cut off the promises of God to them. What we see taking place today with regard to the "new anti-Semitism" strikingly foreshadows what is to come.

How will he relate to the two witnesses?

Just as Satan will have his two witnesses during the end times—the Antichrist and the false prophet—God will have two specially empowered witnesses on earth during this time. God's witnesses and Satan's witnesses will collide in one of the most colossal face-offs of all time. The Lord's two witnesses and their ministry are described in Revelation 11:3-13:

> I will grant authority to my two witnesses, and they will prophesy for twelve hundred and sixty days, clothed in sackcloth. These are the two olive trees and the two lampstands that stand before the Lord of the earth. And if anyone wants to harm them, fire flows out of their mouth and devours their enemies; so if anyone wants to harm them, he must be killed in this way. These have the power to shut up the sky, so that rain will not fall during the days of their prophesying; and they have power over the waters to turn them into blood, and to strike the earth with every plague, as often as they desire.
>
> When they have finished their testimony, the beast

that comes up out of the abyss will make war with them, and overcome them and kill them. And their dead bodies will lie in the street of the great city which mystically is called Sodom and Egypt, where also their Lord was crucified. Those from the peoples and tribes and tongues and nations will look at their dead bodies for three and a half days, and will not permit their dead bodies to be laid in a tomb. And those who dwell on the earth will rejoice over them and celebrate; and they will send gifts to one another, because these two prophets tormented those who dwell on the earth.

But after the three and a half days, the breath of life from God came into them, and they stood on their feet; and great fear fell upon those who were watching them. And they heard a loud voice from heaven saying to them, "Come up here." Then they went up into heaven in the cloud, and their enemies watched them. And in that hour there was a great earthquake, and a tenth of the city fell; seven thousand people were killed in the earthquake, and the rest were terrified and gave glory to the God of heaven.

There are many opinions about the identity of the two witnesses, and I believe the best view is that they will be Elijah and Moses. There are three reasons that Moses is likely one of the two witnesses:

1. Like Moses, these two witnesses will turn the water in rivers to blood and bring other plagues on the earth (Revelation 11:6).

2. On the Mount of Transfiguration, which pictured the second coming glory of Christ, Moses and Elijah appeared with Christ (Matthew 17:1-11).

3. Moses was a prophet.

One specific argument against Moses being one of the two witnesses is that this would mean he would have to die twice. While this is obviously not a common occurrence in history, we have to remember that all of the people in the Bible who were resuscitated back to life—such as Lazarus in John 11—went on to die a second time. So the idea of a person dying twice isn't unheard of in Scripture.

Concerning Elijah, there are five reasons that he is likely one of the two witnesses:

1. Like Enoch, Elijah never tasted physical death.

2. Like Moses, Elijah was present at the transfiguration.

3. Scripture predicts that he will come before "the great and terrible day of the LORD" (Malachi 4:5).

4. God used Elijah to prevent rain from falling for three-and-a-half years, and God will use the two witnesses to do the same.

5. Like the two witnesses, Elijah was a prophet.

Another bit of strong evidence in favor of identifying the two witnesses as Moses and Elijah is that they are mentioned in tandem in the final chapter of the Old Testament (Malachi 4:4-5). And, as we just noted, the two appeared with Jesus on the Mount of Transfiguration in an event that showed a preview of Christ in His second-coming glory (Matthew 16:27–17:5; 2 Peter 1:16-18). Because the two witnesses in Revelation 11 will appear in close connection with the future coming of Christ, I believe it's very likely that they are Elijah and Moses.

The lives and ministries of these two giants from the past will deeply intersect with the reign of the Antichrist and his false prophet. The two witnesses will be given incredible power by God, who says, "I will grant authority to my two witnesses... These have the power to shut up the sky, so that rain will not fall during the days of their prophesying; and they have power over the waters to turn them into blood, and to strike the earth with every plague, as often as they desire" (Revelation 11:3,6). Based on those words, I believe that the two witnesses are the human instruments God will use to call forth the first six trumpets judgments in Revelation 8–9, just as Moses called forth the terrible plagues on Egypt. The Antichrist and false prophet will be able to do counterfeit miracles (just as Pharaoh's magicians were able to), but ultimately they won't be able to match the power of God's two witnesses.

As you can imagine, God's two witnesses will be despised by the Antichrist and his henchman. The world will hate them and conspire against them as they call down judgment after judgment from heaven. Everyone will want them dead. A high price will be put on their heads. They would be instantly murdered if not for the supernatural protection of God for a period of three-and-a-half years. During that span of time they will be invincible. "And if anyone wants to harm them, fire flows out of their mouth and devours their enemies; so if anyone wants to harm them, he must be killed in this way" (Revelation 11:5).

But after the two witnesses have finished their three-and-a-half-year ministry, God will allow the Antichrist to kill them. "When they have finished their testimony, the beast that comes up out of the abyss will make war with them, and overcome them and kill them" (Revelation 11:7). (By the way, keep in mind that our times are in God's hand as well. We too are invincible until the Lord is finished with us and we have completed our work here on earth for Him. What a comforting, strengthening truth that is!)

When the two witnesses are killed, the whole world will rejoice over their deaths. Led by the Antichrist, everyone will celebrate in ghoulish delight and vindictive glee at the deaths of these wit - nesses. "The peoples and tribes and tongues and nations will look at their dead bodies for three and half days, and will not permit their dead bodies to be laid in a tomb. And those who dwell on the earth will rejoice over them and celebrate; and they will send gifts to one another, because these two prophets tormented those who dwell on the earth" (Revelation 11:9-10).

The two witnesses will have been a constant irritant and nagging thorn in the Antichrist's side. As Ray Stedman noted,

> They keep telling the truth to people who want only to embrace their delusions. They keep blunting the Antichrist's carefully concocted propaganda...The vile and godless society of the world under the Antichrist takes the death of the two witnesses as a cause for global celebration. One is reminded of a saying that was common among ancient Roman generals, "The corpse of an enemy always smells sweet!"[35]

People all over the world will be so ecstatic that the two witnesses are dead that they will hold a Christmas-like celebration and send gifts to one another. It will be what we might call "the "Devil's Christmas" or "a satanic Christmas." Interestingly, this is the only mention of any kind of rejoicing or celebration on earth during the entire Tribulation period. People will be so thrilled to see these men dead that no burial will be allowed. They will want to watch their bodies rot in the street.

But the worldwide party over the deaths of the two witnesses won't last long. Amazingly, after the bodies of the two witnesses have laid swelling in the sun for three-and-a-half days, the Lord will raise them back to life before a horror-stricken world. Their resurrection and rapture straight to heaven is vividly described in Revelation 11:11-12: "After three and a half days the breath of life from God came into them, and they stood on their feet; and great fear fell upon those who were beholding them. And they heard a loud voice from heaven saying, 'Come up here.' And they went up into heaven in the cloud, and their enemies beheld them."

Bible commentator John Phillips aptly describes the stunning event:

> Picture the scene—the sun-drenched streets of Jerusalem, the holiday crowd flown in from the ends of the earth for a firsthand look at the corpses of these detested men, the troops in the Beast's uniform, the temple police. There they are, devilish men from every kingdom under heaven, come to dance and feast at the triumph of the Beast. And then it happens! As the crowds strain at the police cordon to peer curiously at the two dead bodies, there comes a sudden change. Their color changes from cadaverous hue to the blooming, rosy glow of youth. Those stiff, stark limbs—they bend, they move! Oh, what a sight! They rise! The crowds fall back, break, and form again.[36]

What a scene that will be! People all over the earth will see the two witnesses caught up to heaven on their favorite TV newscast and listen intently as the analysts attempt to explain what just happened. Revelation 11:9,11-12 makes this brief statement almost in passing about the fact the entire world will witness the death and resurrection of the two witnesses: "The peoples and tribes and tongues and nations will look at their dead bodies for three and half days…But after the three and a half days, the breath of life from God came into them, and they stood on their feet…Then they went up into heaven in the cloud, and their enemies watched them." That everyone around the globe will see this doesn't seem amazing to us today because we're used to instant media accessibility 24/7. But we have to remember the apostle John penned those words almost 2000 years ago. As Tim LaHaye says:

> Ours is the first generation that can literally see the fulfillment of [Revelation] 11:9 in allowing people of the entire world to see such an awesome spectacle. This is one more indication that we are coming closer to the end of the age, because it would have been humanly impossible just a few years ago for the entire world to see these two witnesses in the streets at a given moment of time.[37]

When the Antichrist murders the two witnesses, he will think that his troubles are finally over and that the devastating judgments they inflicted upon the earth have ended. But when he sees the dead, bloated bodies of his archenemies rise from the ground and ascend into heaven, I cannot help but wonder if, even for a brief moment, he becomes afraid at the thought that his reign will eventually be brought to an end.

Are there any historical figures or "types" who foreshadow Antichrist's career?

As we have already seen, Antiochus Epiphanes serves as a clear Old Testament foreshadow of the Antichrist. Some people have discerned additional prototypes of the Antichrist or proto-Antichrist in other individuals who appear in the Bible. Let's consider a few of the most prominent ones:

Nimrod

The first world ruler after the flood is often pointed to as a type of the Antichrist. Nimrod ruled the whole world and built Babel

(Babylon) and the Tower of Babel. The final world ruler will also rule the world and will also be closely associated with Babylon in the end times (Revelation 17–18).

Pharaoh

Pharaoh was the first great oppressor of the Jewish people. He also had court magicians who were able, at least for a while, to match Moses and Aaron miracle for miracle.[38] As Kim Riddlebarger notes, "Their miracle-working power in response to God's messengers clearly anticipates the beast coming out of the earth of Revelation 13:11-17, who performs great and miraculous signs to deceive the inhabitants of the earth so that they worship the beast and his image."[39]

Because the Pharaoh refused to let the Jewish people go, God sent mighty plagues upon Egypt. We see similarly mighty judgments take place during the last days in Revelation 6–11. And when final victory came for Israel and the Pharaoh's army was drowned in the Red Sea, the people triumphantly sang the Song of Moses. This song will be sung again in heaven as the final seven plagues are poured out on the earth in Revelation 15:1-8. Pharaoh's humiliating defeat is a striking foreshadow of the fall of the Antichrist.

Nebuchadnezzar

Nebuchadnezzar was the first world ruler of the "times of the Gentiles." First in time. First in might. In the great statue in Daniel 2, his kingdom is represented by the head of gold. In Daniel 7, his kingdom was portrayed by the mighty lion, the king of the beasts. And on the other end of the spectrum, Antichrist will be the final and most powerful ruler of the "times of the Gentiles."

Nebuchadnezzar erected a great image or idol that all the world had to bow down to or face death (Daniel 3). Interestingly, the image was 60 cubits high and 6 cubits wide. Notice the repetitions of the sixes, as with the number 666. Likewise, the Antichrist will construct a great image that all will be forced to worship or face death. And just as Shadrach, Meshach, and Abednego refused to bow to Nebuchadnezzar's image, in the end times there will be a remnant of people who will refuse to bow to the Antichrist's image.

Nebuchadnezzar was inflated by pride and had to be brought low by the humbling power of God. He was turned into a wild animal for seven years (Daniel 4). So too the Antichrist will be humbled under the mighty hand of God.

Others could be mentioned as proto-Antichrists. Satan attempted to make strides toward world domination through the Roman Caesars. He tried again with Napoleon. Then Hitler. Then Stalin.

When the Antichrist does finally come, he will possess the full power and fury and characteristics of all the aforementioned prototypes. As John Phillips says in reference to Revelation 13:1-3,

> The lion symbolized the empire in Babylon, the bear stood for the Medo-Persian Empire, and the leopard signified Greece. Just as the Roman Empire gathered into itself the Macedonian swiftness of conquest, the Persian tenacity of purpose and the Babylonian appetite for conquest, so will this Beast, the last of a notable line, gather up the characteristics and imperial lust of all three. He is heir of the ages, the last and worst of all the Caesars, Genghis Khans, Napoleons, Hitlers, and Stalins who have plagued this sin-cursed earth. He is the last Gentile claimant to the throne of the world, heir and successor of Nebuchadnezzar, to whom that throne was given long centuries ago.[40]

Will the Antichrist be under God's control?

As Daniel and the book of Revelation reveal, the Antichrist will be the epitome of evil. He will be indwelt and controlled by Satan himself. Some might wonder if God will have any control over the Antichrist's actions, or if he will be free to do whatever he pleases. As we read Revelation 13 we dare not miss a little four-word phrase that appears six times—"was given to him."

Revelation 13:5a	"there *was given to him* a mouth speaking arrogant words"
Revelation 13:5b	"authority to act for forty-two months *was given to him*"
Revelation 13:7a	"it *was...given to him* to make war with the saints"
Revelation 13:7b	"authority over every tribe and people and tongue and nation *was given to him*"
Revelation 13:14	"the signs which it *was given him to* perform"
Revelation 13:15	"it *was given to him* to give breath to the image of the beast"

Antichrist and his henchman, the false prophet, do nothing on their own. Everything is under the control of God's sovereign hand—their actions, words, duration, and miracles. As powerful as the Antichrist is, his power will be a limited, delegated power. Just as in the Old Testament book of Job, Satan and the Antichrist will only be able to do the things that God allows. The Antichrist will wreak horrible havoc in the world, but it's comforting to know that God will remain in control even during earth's darkest hour. No one and nothing can exceed the boundaries He has set in His own wisdom.

Top 10 Keys to Antichrist's Identity

1. He will not be recognized until after the rapture of believers to heaven.

2. He will have obscure beginnings and then rise to world prominence as the pied piper of international peace.

3. He will be a Gentile world leader from the geographical area of the Roman Empire.

4. He will rule over the reunited Roman Empire (the "Unholy" Roman Empire).

5. He will make a seven-year peace covenant with Israel.

6. He will be assassinated and come back to life.

7. He will break his treaty with Israel at the midpoint of the Tribulation and invade the land.

8. He will sit in the Temple of God and declare himself to be God.

9. He will desecrate the Temple in Jerusalem by having an image of himself placed in it.

10. He will rule the world politically, economically, and religiously for three-and-a-half years.

PART 5

The Consummation of the Antichrist

———○———

"Let all Your enemies perish, O LORD;
but let those who love Him be like the
rising of the sun in its might."

JUDGES 5:31

Antichrist and Armageddon:
What will happen?

God's Word is very specific about the demise and doom of the coming Antichrist. Two key passages in the New Testament spell out how he meets his end.

Second Thessalonians 2:8 tells us "the Lord will slay [the Antichrist] with the breath of His mouth." The Lord Jesus Christ will destroy the Antichrist simply by His spoken word at His glorious second coming back to earth. All that will be necessary is for the Lord to speak forth the Antichrist's doom, and it will immediately be so.

Revelation 19:19-21 further reveals that when Christ returns, the Antichrist will be singled for a uniquely quick and severe judgment:

> I saw the beast and the kings of the earth and their armies assembled to make war against Him who sat on the horse and against His army. And the beast was seized, and with him the false prophet who performed the signs in his presence, by which he deceived those who had received the mark of the beast and those who worshiped his image; these two were thrown alive into the lake of fire which burns with brimstone. And the rest were killed with the sword which came from the mouth of Him who sat on the horse, and all the birds were filled with their flesh.

In what is known as the battle of Armageddon, the Antichrist will have gathered all the armies of the earth in the land of Israel. We aren't told in Scripture the exact reason for this gathering of the nations. It could be to destroy Israel once and for all. It could be to challenge Christ at His coming. Or it could be that the nations are gathered there to confront Antichrist, whose kingdom will begin to disintegrate as the world plunges into chaos as a result of the judgments of God as the trumpet judgments (Revelation 8–11) and bowl judgments (Revelation 16) are poured out.

Whatever the reason for the gathering, the troops will muster at Armageddon in northern Israel, and then the campaign will spread out over the entire length of Israel from Armageddon in the north to Edom in the southern part of modern-day Jordan. Caught in the middle of this conflagration will be Jerusalem (Zechariah 12:1-3). As the campaign rages and it looks like Israel will finally be wiped off the face of the earth, Jesus will come in power and great glory.

When Christ returns, He will destroy all the armies gathered at Armageddon with the sharp sword of His word that proceeds from His mouth. All He will have to do to destroy all of man's military might is simply say, "Drop dead," and the armies of the world will melt before Him like wax. However, the Antichrist and the false prophet will not be killed like the others. They will be thrown alive "into the lake of fire and brimstone," where they will be joined 1000 years later by Satan, the head of this false trinity (Revelation 20:10). It's at this point we notice a rather interesting parallel: Two men in the Old Testament went to heaven without dying—Enoch and Elijah. And two men in the New Testament will go to hell without dying—Antichrist and the false prophet.

This is the final doom of the devil's masterpiece. His false kingdom will be swept away and the glorious kingdom of Christ will be established. Daniel 7:26 is a powerful reminder that the Antichrist's termination is absolutely certain: "The court will sit for judgment, and his dominion will be taken away, annihilated and destroyed forever."

Is the Antichrist alive today?

The world today is looking for a leader. With growing dangers and uncertainties everywhere and the global economy spiraling downward, people everywhere are hungry for leadership and direction unlike any other time in human history. The world's prospects for the future are gloomy and getting worse. Everyone knows it. And everyone knows that we need someone who can offer hope and chart a clear course for solving the world's mounting crises. Arnold Toynbee wisely noted, "The nations are ready to give the kingdoms of the world to any one man who will offer us a solution to our world's problems."[1] In *Forbes* magazine, Paul Johnson, an eminent British historian, said, "There's one lesson to be learned above all others: There is no substitute for prudent, strong and courageous leadership. This is what the civilized world currently lacks and must find—soon."[2] The Bible predicts that just such a leader is coming. In fact, he may already be here.

Amazingly, in a 1999 *Newsweek* poll 19 percent of Americans said they believe that the Antichrist is on earth now. That's one in five Americans who believe that the Antichrist is alive and in our midst. And in the same poll, nearly half of those who accept biblical prophecy as trustworthy believe he is alive now.[3] Could they be right?

In response to this often-asked question, I want to offer three key thoughts.

First, I want to make it crystal clear that I don't believe anyone can say for sure that the Antichrist is alive today. I believe, based on 2 Thessalonians 2:3-7, that the identity of the Antichrist will not be revealed until after believers have been raptured to glory and seen the Lord Jesus face-to-face. So if you are trying to figure out whether some particular person in Washington, DC, London, Paris, or Rome is the Antichrist, you are wasting your time. The Bible never identifies the Antichrist by name, and it never tells us to try to identify him. The number 666, the number of his name, will not become discernible until after the rapture. According to Scripture, the Antichrist will be revealed after the rapture of the church, after the removal of the restraining power of the Holy Spirit (2 Thessalonians 2:3-7). He will emerge on the world scene when he makes his peace covenant with Israel (Daniel 9:27). That will be his formal introduction to the world, and that won't take place until *after* God's people are in heaven.

Second, while no one knows if *the* Antichrist is alive today, we can be certain that *an* antichrist is alive in the world at this very moment. Writing late in the first century AD, the apostle John said that "the spirit of the antichrist" was already at work undermining and opposing the work of God (1 John 4:3; see also 2:18). So we can be certain that the *spirit* of Antichrist is alive and well today. The apostle Paul also said that in his day, Satan was already at work trying to bring the Antichrist onto the world scene (2 Thessalonians 2:6-7).

I believe that in every generation, Satan has a man—a satanically prepared vessel—ready to take center stage and rule the world. After all, this is Satan's goal (Isaiah 14:12-14). Satan wants to be worshiped as God. And because God has stated that He will rule the world through His Son, the Christ, Satan's goal is to usurp God and rule the world through his man, the Antichrist. The problem for Satan is that he doesn't know when the coming of Christ will occur. That's why he likely has someone prepared in every generation who will try to take over the world and stand against Christ and the establishment of His glorious kingdom. Satan is left guessing when the rapture might occur, so he must have a man in every generation whom he is ready to indwell as he waits on God's timing.

If that truly is the case, then that means Satan has someone alive today whom he will use to usurp the rightful place of the King of kings if the situation presents itself. There is always *an* Antichrist ready somewhere. But Satan cannot bring his program to fruition because the restraining power of the Holy Spirit is holding him back. Eventually, in God's timing, the restrainer will be taken out of the way and Satan will be allowed to put his long-awaited agenda into action (2 Thessalonians 2:6-7).

Third, while I want to reemphasize that no one can say for sure whether *the* Antichrist is alive today, I wouldn't be surprised if he is. Many of the key pieces to the prophetic puzzle for the last days seem to be coming together. We have the United States of Europe coming together before our eyes in the form of the European

Union. Globalism is here, and the advanced technology necessary for setting up a one-world government and economy already exists. Crises of epic proportion are erupting with sobering frequency and regularity, paving the way for more and more change. The world is ripe for a great peacemaker, especially one who can bring peace to the Middle East.

Again, no one can say for sure that the Antichrist is alive right now. But think about it: If Jesus' second coming is likely to happen within the next 40–50 years, then the Antichrist is almost certainly alive somewhere right now. While the Bible never tells us how old Antichrist will be when he comes onto the world scene, we can probably safely assume he will be at least in his forties or fifties, if not older. Moreover, while I am *not* saying that Jesus is coming in the next 40–50 years (because no one knows the time of His return), I do think it's highly probable. If that's the case, then the Antichrist is alive somewhere on the earth today. He may even be on the world political scene, waiting in the wings for his moment. Ed Hindson warns, "Someone ominous is looming on the horizon of human existence. He may still be in the shadows for the moment, but he could suddenly burst forth on the scene at any time."[4]

Prophecy teacher Gary Frazier paints this chilling picture:

> Somewhere at this moment there may be a young man growing to maturity. He is in all likelihood a brooding, thoughtful young man. Inside his heart, however, there is hellish rage. It boils like a cauldron of molten lead. He hates God. He despises Jesus Christ. He detests the Church. In his mind there is taking shape the form of a dream of conquest. He will disingenuously present himself as a friend of Christ and the Church. Yet…he will,

once empowered, pour out hell itself onto this world. Can the world produce such a prodigy? Hitler was once a little boy. Stalin was a lad. Nero was a child. The tenderness of childhood will be shaped by the devil into the terror of the *antichrist*.[5]

Again, all the indicators that the end times are on the horizon seem to be coming together. The emergence of Antichrist could take place very soon. Which would mean the coming of the Lord is even closer.

Are you ready to meet Him at His coming?

How does this apply to your life today?

I'll never forget seeing the movie *The Omen* for the first time in 1976 while I was in high school. The movie was remade a few years ago, but the original is still a classic. While the movie is a fictional horror film, its basic theme is sound: The Antichrist is coming, and he may even be alive and walking the earth right now. Though the movie itself is fiction, its warning is very real. Antichrist and his one-world religious and economic system are coming.

There is a gripping scene that takes place early in the movie. On the morning after the nightmarish fifth birthday party for Damien (the Antichrist), a Catholic priest named Father Brennan pays an unannounced visit to the office of Ambassador Thorn (Damien's father). As soon as Father Brennan is alone with Thorn, he blurts out a startling warning to the ambassador, desperately urging him to accept Christ as his Savior *now*.

Ambassador Thorn is stunned as the priest proceeds to tell him that his young son is really the son of Satan—the Antichrist. Thorn is incensed and calls for security guards to haul the priest away. At the time, Thorn considers Father Brennan's warning to be foolish. Interestingly, however, even when Thorn finally does realize that Damien is the Antichrist, he still refuses to accept Christ. Father Brennan's warning is still applicable today. Have you accepted Christ while there is still opportunity?

Scripture teaches that when the Antichrist appears, most people will still refuse to accept Christ. Instead, they will turn to follow the lawless one. Second Thessalonians 2:8-12 says,

> Then [the] lawless one will be revealed whom the Lord will slay with the breath of His mouth and bring to an end by the appearance of His coming; that is, the one whose coming is in accord with the activity of Satan, with all power and signs and false wonders, and with all the deception of wickedness for those who perish, because they did not receive the love of the truth so as to be saved. For this reason God will send upon them a deluding influence so that they will believe what is false, in order that they all may be judged who did not believe the truth, but took pleasure in wickedness.

If you are not yet a Christian, don't count on the fact that you still have time to wait and receive Christ later. No one knows when he or she might die, and we certainly don't know when the rapture will occur. So if you've put off making a decision, don't put it off any longer. Accept Jesus Christ as your Savior now!

The Bible tells us that when Jesus Christ died on the cross, He purchased a full pardon from the penalty of sin for you and me. The pardon has been bought and paid for, and God offers it to every person. All we have to do to make this pardon effective in our lives is simply to receive it, to accept it. John 1:12 says, "As many as received Him, to them He gave the right to become children of God, even to those who believe in His name."

Why not do it now?

If you already know the Savior, the challenge for you is to live in light of what you know. Though the end times are still future, what we've been reading in this book has practical applications for today.

First, we must avoid trying to set dates for the Lord's coming and attempting to identify the Antichrist. And we should not listen to those who claim to know these things. The times are in God's hand alone, and He has not chosen to reveal this information to anyone on earth. As Jesus said, "Heaven and earth will pass away, but My words will not pass away. But of that day and hour no one knows, not even the angels of heaven, nor the Son, but the Father alone" (Matthew 24:35-36). And after Jesus arose from the dead, when the disciples asked when He would restore the kingdom to Israel, He said, "It is not for you to know times or epochs which the Father has fixed by His own authority" (Acts 1:7).

Second, knowing about the Antichrist and how events in our world today seem set up for his arrival should motivate us to live each day for Jesus Christ and others. We don't know how much time we have before Christ raptures His church, but it could happen anytime. That's the message of the New Testament. And before Antichrist comes, Christ will come. We are to be "looking for the blessed hope" and living with it in view (Titus 2:13). We need to make sure we're living our lives in a way that will please the Lord, for He could come at any time. My friend Randall Price says it well:

> What good is to be able to understand the seven
> heads described in Revelation 13:1 if we don't use our
> own head? Of what profit is it to discern the ten toes

of Daniel 2:42-44; 7:74 if we don't move our own two feet? And what value is it to know about the great mouth that speaks lies (Daniel 7:8; Revelation 13:5), unless we open our mouth and speak the truth? In every generation where prophecy has been properly proclaimed, the results have been a harvest of souls to the glory of God.[6]

Third, in these times of deepening fear and surging uncertainty, when the storm clouds seem to be gathering on the horizon, we need to be filled with hope. We need to put on the helmet of salvation (Ephesians 6:17) and realize that the only hope for this world—and the only hope for us—is the coming of Jesus Christ.

Kim Riddlebarger offers this sage advice for our time—may we each take it to heart:

> Instead of fearing and dreading the Antichrist and worrying about the latest events in the Middle East or whether the number 666 appears on a household product ID, we should be longing for the second coming of Jesus Christ. For Satan and his cronies have already been defeated by the blood and righteousness of Jesus, although for a short time they will run amuck because they know their time is short. Regarding the fate of our enemy, Martin Luther perhaps said it best: "One little word shall fell him." Amen. Even so, come quickly, Lord Jesus![7]

Notes

Part 1: The Curiosity About the Antichrist

1. "'Scary' Harris poll: 24% of Republicans think Obama 'may be the Antichrist,'" www.news.yahoo.com/s/dailybeast/20100323/ts.../7269 _scarynewgoppoll.

2. Daniel B. Wallace, "Is Obama the Antichrist?" *The Christian Post,* August 20, 2009, www.christianpost.com/article/.../is-obama-the -antichrist/.

3. Daniel B. Wallace, "Is Obama the Antichrist?"

4. At http://answers.yahoo.com/question/index?qid=20090122184810 AAkh6XI.

5. Mark Hosenball and Michael Isikoff, "Extremist Reaction," *Newsweek* (April 12, 2010), 14.

6. "The Dajjal: Islam's Antichrist," www.answering islam.org/Authors/ JR/.../ch08_the_dajjal.htm.

7. Denis the Carthusian, *Dialogue on the Catholic Faith* 6, in *Opera omnia,* vol. 18 (Tournai: n.p., 1899), 468.

8. H.L. Willmington, *The King Is Coming* (Wheaton, IL: Tyndale House, 1981), 81.

9. John MacArthur Jr., *Revelation 12–22* (Chicago: Moody Press, 2000), 51.

10. Thomas Ice and Timoth Demy, *The Truth About the Antichrist and His Kingdom* (Eugene, OR: Harvest House, 1996), 40-41.

11. Gary DeMar, *End Times Fiction* (Nashville, TN: Thomas Nelson, 2001), 134-37.

12. *Didache* 16. 4. DeMar maintains that the false messiahs in Mark 13:22 were present in the days before the destruction of the temple in AD 70 and that Nero was the Beast of Revelation 13. But the *Didache,* which was written after AD 70 refers to a future individual who will fulfill these prophecies.

13. Irenaeus, *Against Heresies* 5.28.2.

14. Irenaeus, *Against Heresies* 5.30.2.

15. Irenaeus, *Against Heresies* 5.25.3-4.

16. Hippolytus, *Antichrist* 6. Cf. Bernard McGinn, *Antichrist: Two Thousand Years of Human Fascination with Evil* (San Francisco: HarperSanFrancisco, 1994), 61.

17. McGinn, *Antichrist: Two Thousand Years of Human Fascination with Evil* (San Francisco: HarperSanFrancisco, 1994), 61.

18. McGinn, *Antichrist: Two Thousand Years of Human Fascination with Evil,* 63.

19. Cyril, *Catechetical Lectures* 15.12-15.

20. Jerome, Commentary on Daniel 7:8; 11:39; 11:45. Unlike most of the other early writers, Jerome did not support the view that the Antichrist would rebuild the Temple in Jerusalem. He also strongly rejected any idea of a literal 1000-year reign of Christ. But he did believe in a future, personal Antichrist. Jerome believed that Daniel 7–11, 2 Thessalonians 2, Matthew 24, Revelation 17, and John 5:43 all related to the future Antichrist. John Chrysostom also rejected the idea of a rebuilt Temple, but he too believed in a personal Antichrist in the end times. *Homily 3 on 2 Thess.*

21. McGinn, *Antichrist: Two Thousand Years of Human Fascination with Evil,* 63.

22. Ibid., 78.

23. Kim Riddlebarger, *The Man of Sin: Uncovering the Truth About the Antichrist* (Grand Rapids: Baker, 2006), 10.

24. Robert C. Fuller, *Naming the Antichrist: History of an American Obsession* (New York: Oxford Press, 1995), 34-35.

25. G. Salmon, *An Historical Introduction to the Study of the Books of the New Testament,* 9th ed. (London: John Murray, 1904), 230-31.

26. There are at least 11 different views on the identity of the restrainer in 2 Thessalonians 2: (1) the Roman Empire, (2) the Jewish State, (3) the apostle Paul, (4) the preaching of the gospel, (5) human government, (6) Satan, (7) Elijah, (8) some unknown heavenly being, (9) Michael the archangel, (10) the Holy Spirit, and (11) the church.

27. Donald Grey Barnhouse, *Thessalonians: An Expositional Commentary* (Grand Rapids: Zondervan, 1977), 99-100.

28. Ed Hindson, *Is the Antichrist Alive and Well?* (Eugene, OR: Harvest House, 1998), 22.

Part 2: The Character of the Antichrist

1. Grant R. Jeffrey, *Prince of Darkness* (Toronto: Frontier Research Publications, 1994), 29.

2. Ibid., 30.

3. A.W. Pink, *The Antichrist* (Swengel, PA: Bible Truth Depot, 1923; reprint, Grand Rapids: Kregel, 1988), 62.

4. J. Dwight Pentecost, *Will Man Survive?* (Grand Rapids: Zondervan, 1971), 93.

5. H.L. Willmington, *The King Is Coming,* rev. ed. (Wheaton, IL: Tyndale House, 1981), 66-67.

6. Hank Hanegraaff, "Who is the Antichrist?" www.ptm.org/05PT/Sep Oct/antiChrist.pdf.

7. Gary DeMar, *End Times Fiction* (Nashville, TN: Thomas Nelson, 2001), 137.

8. DeMar, *End Times Fiction,* 140.

9. DeMar, *End Times Fiction,* 137.

10. The verb "is coming" in 1 John 2:18 is a futuristic present that "assumes the future coming of the antichrist to be as certain as the present reality." D. Edmond Hiebert, *The Epistles of John* (Greenville, SC: Bob Jones University Press, 1991), 109.

11. Here is a small sampling of the scholars who believe 1 John speaks of a future personal Antichrist: F.F. Bruce, *The Epistles of John* (Grand Rapids: Eerdmans, 1992), 64-68; Martyn Lloyd-Jones, *Walking with God: Life in Christ,* vol. 2 (Wheaton, IL: Crossway, 1993), 98-101; R.C.H.

Lenski, *The Interpretation of the Epistles of St. Peter, St. John and St. Jude* (Minneapolis: Augsburg, 1966), 430-32; James Montgomery Boice, *The Epistles of John* (Grand Rapids: Zondervan, 1979), 84-86; Simon J. Kistemaker, *James and I–III John,* New Testament Commentary (Grand Rapids: Baker, 1986), 275-76; I. Howard Marshall, *The Epistles of John,* The New International Commentary on the New Testament, gen. ed. F.F. Bruce (Grand Rapids: Eerdmans, 1978), 148-51; John R.W. Stott, *The Letters of John,* rev. ed., Tyndale New Testament Commentaries (Grand Rapids: Eerdmans, 1994), 108-10; D. Edmond Hiebert, *The Epistles of John,* 106-09. The only respected evangelical scholar I could find who did not hold that 1 John 2:18 refers to the coming of a future personal Antichrist was Brooke Foss Westcott, who wrote in the nineteenth century. And even then Westcott was not decisive. He said the passage is "not decisive as to St. John's teaching in regard to the coming of one great Antichrist, of which the others were preparatory embodiments." B.F. Westcott, *The Epistles of John* (Grand Rapids: Eerdmans, 1966), 70. Bernard McGinn, who is not an evangelical Christian, wrote a masterpiece on the subject of Antichrist and says that the use of the singular for antichrist in 1 John "made it possible for most later Christians to believe in many antichrists as well as in the single final opposer predicted in 2 Thessalonians and the Apocalypse." Bernard McGinn, *Antichrist: Two Thousand Years of the Human Fascination with Evil* (San Francisco: HarperSanFrancisco, 1994), 56.

12. James Montgomery Boice, *The Epistles of John: An Expositional Commentary* (Grand Rapids: Zondervan, 1979), 86.

13. F.F. Bruce, *The Epistles of John* (reprint, Grand Rapids: Eerdmans, 1992), 65.

14. Kim Riddlebarger, *The Man of Sin: Uncovering the Truth about the Antichrist* (Grand Rapids: Baker, 2006), 13.

15. Ed Hindson, *Is the Antichrist Alive and Well?* (Eugene, OR: Harvest House, 1998), 19.

16. Pink, *The Antichrist,* 79.

17. John Phillips, *Exploring Revelation* (Neptune, NJ: Loizeaux Brothers, 1991), 166.

18. Pink, *The Antichrist,* 81.

19. Willmington, *The King Is Coming,* 95.

20. John Phillips, *Exploring the Future: A Comprehensive Guide to Bible Prophecy* (Grand Rapids: Kregel, 2003), 272.

21. Robert L. Thomas, *Revelation 1–7* (Chicago: Moody Press, 1992), 481.

22. Arnold G. Fruchtenbaum, *The Footsteps of the Messiah,* rev. ed. (Tustin, CA: Ariel Ministries, 2003), 211.

23. Fruchtenbaum, *The Footsteps of the Messiah,* 211.

24. Lehman Strauss, *The Book of the Revelation* (Neptune, NJ: Loizeaux Brothers, 1964), 249.

25. Strauss, *The Book of the Revelation,* 249.

26. Pink, *The Antichrist,* 60-61.

27. Gary DeMar accuses those who believe in a future, individual Antichrist of amalgamating divergent entities to "build an Antichrist." Gary DeMar, *End Times Fiction* (Nashville, TN: Thomas Nelson, 2001), 135-36. What DeMar ignores is that most scholars, even those who would disagree with many aspects of the overall end-time view presented in this book, agree that all these passages and titles refer to the Antichrist. For instance, D. Martyn Lloyd-Jones said, "It is very clear that other writers in different places are concerned about exactly the same thing. Second Thessalonians 2, again, is clearly a description of the same person, the same power, and the same condition. Then in Daniel 7–11 you will find clear descriptions of the same thing, and of course there is another classic passage in Revelation where you get an account of the two beasts, the one arising out of the sea and other arising out of the earth. All these are clearly references to the same power." D. Martyn Lloyd-Jones, *Walking with God* (Wheaton, IL: Crossway, 1993), 98. A.W. Pink notes, "Instead of apportioning these names to different persons, we must see that they denominate the same individual, only in different relationships, or as giving us different phases of his character" (*The Antichrist,* 61). Futurists haven't manufactured an Antichrist. We have simply brought together all the relevant texts about him.

28. Joel Richardson, *Antichrist: Islam's Awaited Messiah* (Enumclaw, WA: Pleasant Word, 2006), 52-70.

29. Richardson, *Antichrist: Islam's Awaited Messiah,* 67-68.

30. David R. Reagan, "The Antichrist: Will He Be a Muslim?" www.prophezine.com/…/TheAntichristWillhebeaMuslim/…/Default.aspx.

31. Richardson, *Antichrist: Islam's Awaited Messiah*, 198.

32. Richardson, *Antichrist: Islam's Awaited Messiah*, 101-2. One of Richardson's arguments is based on Ezekiel 39:17, which says, "Thus says the Lord GOD, 'Are you the one of whom I spoke in former days through My servants the prophets of Israel, who prophesied in those days for many years that I would bring you against them?'" His argument goes like this: "The question must be asked then, if Gog and Magog are spoken of by Israel's former prophets prior to Ezekiel, then where are all these references? One will be very hard pressed to find any unless one does some serious stretching of the Scriptures. But if we take the position that Gog is Antichrist, then it is very easy to find numerous passages about Antichrist and his invading Army throughout the prophets" (102). I don't believe it takes any stretching of Scripture to find references to a great northern invasion of Israel. Daniel 11:40 refers to the "king of the North," whom I equate with Gog. Daniel 11 was written after Ezekiel, but Daniel was a contemporary of Ezekiel during the Babylonian captivity. The "northern army" in Joel 2:20 could also be a reference to this invasion. Or Ezekiel 38:17 may not refer to any specific prior prophecy. Charles Feinberg noted, "It is possible that there is no direct reference to any specific group of prophecies but to a general concept that permeates prophecy. Earlier prophets, in speaking of eschatological times, foretold catastrophic events and God's judgment on Israel's enemies, though the specific name of Gog did not appear in their prophecies." Charles Lee Feinberg, *The Prophecy of Ezekiel: The Glory of the Lord* (Chicago: Moody Press, 1969), 225. I don't believe that Ezekiel 38:17 is as big an obstacle to my view as Richardson contends.

33. DeMar, *End Times Fiction*, 142-45; Kenneth Gentry, *The Beast of Revelation* (Tyler, TX: Institute for Christian Economics, 1989).

34. Riddlebarger, *The Man of Sin: Uncovering the Truth about the Antichrist*, 11.

35. Kenneth Gentry, *The Beast of Revelation* (Tyler, TX: Institute for Christian Economics, 1989), 35. O. Ruhle says that the 616 variant was an attempt to link Gaius Caesar (Caligula) to the beast out of the sea in Revelation 13. The numerical value of his name in Greek equals 616. Gerhard Kittel, ed., *The Theological Dictionary of the New Testament*, trans. Geoffrey W. Bromiley, vol. 1 (Grand Rapids: Eerdmans, 1964), 462-63.

36. Gentry, *The Beast of Revelation*, 53-54.

37. For a thorough discussion about the date when Revelation was written, see Mark Hitchcock, "The Stake in the Heart: The A.D. 95 Date of Revelation" in *The End Times Controversy* (Eugene, OR: Harvest House, 2003), 123-50.

38. Robert L. Thomas, *Revelation 8–22: An Exegetical Commentary* (Chicago: Moody Press, 1995), 179-80.

39. Many preterists believe that a man named Gessius Florus, the Roman procurator or governor of Judea under Nero, was the false prophet referred to in Revelation 13:11-18. J. Stuart Russell, *The Parousia: The New Testament Doctrine of Our Lord's Second Coming*, new ed. (London: T. Fisher Unwin, 1887; reprint, Grand Rapid: Baker, 1999), 465-69; Kenneth L. Gentry Jr., *He Shall Have Dominion: A Postmillennial Eschatology* (Tyler, TX: Institute for Christian Economics, 1992), 410. Yet neither Russell nor Gentry provide any historical evidence that Gessius Florus ever performed great signs and wonders, that he constructed an image of Nero, that he made the image speak, that he forced the mark of the beast upon the populace, or that he executed those who failed to take the mark. Moreover, Josephus, the Jewish historian, mentions Gessius Florus in his writings but never describes any activities by him that even remotely correspond to the prophecies of Revelation 13:11-18. If Florus did perform great signs and wonders or do any of the other things prophesied in Revelation 13, Josephus's failure to mention these stupendous facts is inexplicable. The inability to successfully name a historical person who fulfilled the role and activities of the false prophet in the Neronic era is a major stumbling block for the preterist view of the beast.

40. David E. Aune, *Revelation 6–16*, Word Biblical Commentary, gen. ed. Bruce M. Metzger, vol. 52B (Nashville, TN: Thomas Nelson, 1998), 771.

41. For a complete refutation of the view that Nero is the beast of Revelation 13, see Andy Woods, "Revelation 13 and the First Beast" in *The End Times Controversy* (Eugene, OR: Harvest House, 2003), 237-50.

42. Irenaeus, who wrote in the late second century, suggested three names for the total 666: Evanthas, Lateinos, and Teitan (*Against Heresies* 5.30.3). But he never suggested Nero.

43. Simon J. Kistemaker, *Exposition of the Book of Revelation*, New Testament Commentary (Grand Rapids: Baker, 2001), 395.

44. Thomas, *Revelation 8–22: An Exegetical Commentary*, 185.

45. William F. Arndt and F.W. Gingrich, *A Greek-English Lexicon of the New Testament* (Chicago: University of Chicago Press, 1957), 876.

46. Thomas, *Revelation 8–22: An Exegetical Commentary*, 181.

47. Henry Morris, *Revelation Record* (Wheaton, IL: Tyndale, 1983), 252.

48. Hal Harless, "666: The Beast and His Mark in Revelation 13," *The Conservative Theological Journal* (December 2003): 342-46.

49. Morris, *Revelation Record*, 255.

50. Fruchtenbaum, *The Footsteps of the Messiah*, rev. ed., 255.

51. Fruchtenbaum, *The Footsteps of the Messiah*, rev. ed., 255.

52. John F. Walvoord. *The Prophecy Knowledge Handbook* (Wheaton, IL: SP Publications, 1990), 587.

53. M.R. DeHaan, *Studies in Revelation* (Grand Rapids: Zondervan, 1946; reprint, Grand Rapids: Kregel, 1998), 189.

54. Morris, *Revelation Record*, 256.

55. Morris, *Revelation Record*, 256.

56. The word used for the seal of God on the foreheads of the saints in Revelation 7:3 is the Greek word *sphragizo*, which is used of the invisible seal of the Holy Spirit in the New Testament (2 Corinthians 1:22; Ephesians 1:13; 4:30). The word used for mark (*charagma*), on the other hand, refers to a visible mark, imprint, or etching. Therefore, while God's mark on His saints will be invisible, the beast's mark will be visible.

57. Steven Levy, "Playing the ID Card," *Newsweek* (May 13, 2002), 44-46.

Part 3: The Coming of the Antichrist

1. Charles H. Dyer, *World News and Bible Prophecy* (Wheaton, IL: Tyndale, 1995), 214.

2. W.A. Criswell, *Expository Sermons on Revelation* (Grand Rapids: Zondervan, 1969), 107-8.

3. John MacArthur Jr., *Revelation 12–22* (Chicago: Moody Press, 2000), 36.

4. Randall Price, "The Divine Preservation of the Jewish People," World of the Bible Ministry Update, October 1, 2009, http://www.worldofthebible.com/update.htm.

5. Price, "The Divine Preservation of the Jewish People."

6. Thomas Ice and Timothy Demy, *The Truth About the Signs of the Times* (Eugene, OR: Harvest House, 1997), 37.

7. Randall Price, *The Coming Last Days Temple* (Eugene, OR: Harvest House, 1999), 592.

8. Thomas Ice and Timothy Demy, *Prophecy Watch* (Eugene, OR: Harvest House, 1998), 150.

9. John F. Walvoord, *Major Bible Prophecies: 37 Crucial Prophecies That Affect You Today* (Grand Rapids: Zondervan, 1993), 319.

10. David Jeremiah, *What in the World Is Going On?* (Nashville: Thomas Nelson, 2008), 141-42.

Part 4: The Career of the Antichrist

1. Tim LaHaye and Jerry B. Jenkins, *Left Behind* (Wheaton, IL: Tyndale, 1995), 352, 413.

2. Henry Morris, *Revelation Record* (Wheaton, IL: Tyndale, 1983), 323.

3. Morris, *Revelation Record*, 348-49.

4. John Phillips, *Exploring Revelation* (Neptune, NJ: Loizeaux Brothers, 1991), 167.

5. Warren Wiersbe, *The Bible Exposition Commentary,* New Testament, vol. 2 (Wheaton, IL: Victor Books, 1989), 605.

6. J. Vernon McGee, *Thru the Bible,* vol. 5 (Nashville: Thomas Nelson Publishers, 1983), 1000. Some argue strenuously and stridently against this view. Apologist Hank Hanegraaff deems an actual death and resurrection of the Antichrist as preposterous. He says, "If Antichrist could rise from the dead and control the earth and sky…Christianity would lose the basis for believing that Christ's resurrection vindicated His claim to deity. In a Christian worldview, Satan can parody the work of Christ through 'all kinds of counterfeit miracles, signs and wonders' (2 Thessalonians 2:9), but he cannot perform the truly miraculous as Christ did. If Satan possesses the creative power of God, he could have masqueraded as the resurrected Christ. Moreover, the notion that Satan can perform acts that are indistinguishable from genuine miracles suggests a dualistic worldview in which God and Satan are equal powers competing for dominance." Hank Hanegraaff, *The Apocalypse Code: Find Out What the Bible Really Says About the End Times and Why It Matters Today* (Nashville: Thomas Nelson, 2007),

xix-xx. Hanegraaff further states: "What is at stake here is nothing less than the deity and resurrection of Christ. In a Christian worldview, only God has the power to raise the dead." Hank Hanegraaff and Sigmund Brouwer, *The Last Disciple* (Wheaton, IL: Tyndale, 2004), 394.

7. William F. Arndt and F.W. Gingrich, *A Greek-English Lexicon of the New Testament* (Chicago: University of Chicago Press, 1957), 55.

8. George Abbott-Smith, *A Manual Greek Lexicon of the New Testament*, 3rd ed. (Edinburgh: T. & T. Clark, 1937), 443.

9. Joseph Henry Thayer, *A Greek-English Lexicon of the New Testament* (New York: American Book Company, 1889), 620.

10. Gregory H. Harris, "Satan's Deceptive Miracles in the Tribulation," *Bibliotheca Sacra* (July-September 1999): 310.

11. Harris, "Satan's Deceptive Miracles in the Tribulation," 310.

12. Philip Edgcumbe Hughes, *A Commentary on the Epistle to the Hebrews* (Grand Rapids: Eerdmans, 1977), 80-81.

13. Harris, "Satan's Deceptive Miracles in the Tribulation," 311.

14. Harris, "Satan's Deceptive Miracles in the Tribulation," 311.

15. Harris, "Satan's Deceptive Miracles in the Tribulation," 311.

16. Warren Wiersbe, *The Bible Exposition Commentary*, New Testament, vol. 2 (Wheaton, IL: Victor Books, 1989), 605.

17. Gregory H. Harris, "The Wound of the Beast in the Tribulation," *Bibliotheca Sacra* (October-December 1999): 466.

18. Charles C. Ryrie, *Revelation,* Everyman's Bible Commentary (Chicago: Moody Press, 1968), 83.

19. Harris, "The Wound of the Beast in the Tribulation," 467.

20. J.B. Smith, *A Revelation of Jesus Christ: A Commentary on the Book of Revelation* (Scottsdale, PA: Herald Press, 1961), 467.

21. Harris, "The Wound of the Beast in the Tribulation," 467.

22. John Phillips, *Exploring Revelation* (Neptune, NJ: Loizeaux Brothers, 1991), 119.

23. Harris, "The Wound of the Beast in the Tribulation," 469.

24. Smith, *A Revelation of Jesus Christ: A Commentary on the Book of Revelation*, 195-96.

25. Donald Grey Barnhouse, *Revelation: An Expository Commentary* (Grand Rapids: Zondervan, 1971), 240.

26. Thomas Ice and Timothy Demy, *Fact Facts on Bible Prophecy* (Eugene, OR: Harvest House, 1997), 78-79.

27. Phillips, *Exploring Revelation*, 171.

28. Ice and Demy, *Fact Facts on Bible Prophecy*, 78-79.

29. Arnold G. Fruchtenbaum, *The Footsteps of the Messiah*, rev. ed. (Tustin, CA: Ariel Ministries, 2003), 257.

30. Fruchtenbaum, *The Footsteps of the Messiah*, 256-60.

31. Wiersbe, *The Bible Exposition Commentary*, 606.

32. Daniel 12:11 says that the abomination of desolation will stand in the holy place for 1290 days. That's the final three-and-a-half years of the Tribulation (1260 days) plus 30 extra days. Why an extra 30 days? When Jesus returns at His second coming at the end of the Tribulation, Antichrist will be destroyed, but evidently the image will remain in the Temple for another 30 days beyond that time and then it too will be removed and destroyed.

33. Arthur E. Bloomfield, *How to Recognize the Antichrist: What Bible Prophecy Says About the Great Deceiver* (Minneapolis, MN: Bethany House, 1975), 129-30.

34. Bloomfield, *How to Recognize the Antichrist: What Bible Prophecy Says About the Great Deceiver*, 131-32.

35. Ray C. Stedman, *God's Final Word: Understanding Revelation* (Grand Rapids: Discovery House, 1991), 220.

36. Phillips, *Exploring Revelation*, 150.

37. Tim LaHaye, *Revelation Unveiled* (Grand Rapids: Zondervan, 1999), 188.

38. Kim Riddlebarger, *The Man of Sin: Uncovering the Truth about the Antichrist* (Grand Rapids: Baker, 2006), 45.

39. Riddlebarger, *The Man of Sin: Uncovering the Truth about the Antichrist*, 45.

40. Phillips, *Exploring Revelation*, 163.

Part 5: The Consummation of the Antichrist

1. *Bible Prophecy Basics: The Rise of Antichrist*, at www.angelfire.com/realm/ofstardust/RISE_AC.html.

2. Paul Johnson, "A World in Search of Leaders," *Forbes* (November 24, 2008), 29.

3. *The Daily Oklahoman* (April 12, 2002), 2B.

4. Ed Hindson, *Is the Antichrist Alive and Well?* (Eugene, OR: Harvest House, 1998), 8.

5. Gary Frazier, *Signs of the Coming of Christ* (Arlington, TX: Discovery Ministries, 1998), 149.

6. Randall Price, *Jerusalem in Prophecy* (Eugene, OR: Harvest House, 1998), 50.

7. Kim Riddlebarger, *The Man of Sin: Uncovering the Truth about the Antichrist* (Grand Rapids: Baker, 2006), 178.

CASHLESS

Over 1900 years ago, the Bible predicted that one man, the coming Antichrist, will take control of the entire world's economy. Many have wondered how this could ever happen. We may now have the answer. Mark skillfully brings together current research and Bible prophecy as he addresses how the stage is being set for a cashless society under Antichrist's control.

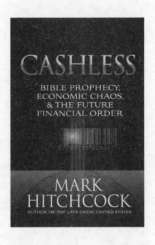

2012, THE BIBLE, AND THE END OF THE WORLD

The ancient Mayans were expert astronomers, and their advanced calendar cycles end on December 21, 2012. This has spurred worldwide speculation that 12/21/12 will be a catastrophic day of apocalypse for the entire globe. But how does this match up to what the Bible says about the future? A fascinating survey that discerns fiction from fact.

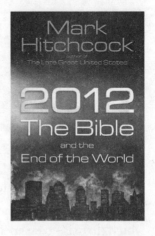

Other Harvest House Books
by Mark Hitchcock

THE AMAZING CLAIMS OF BIBLE PROPHECY

One powerful way to defend the reliability of the Bible is to look at the hundreds of prophecies that have been fulfilled with 100 percent accuracy. That track record means we can trust everything Scripture says about what is still future. As you trace the amazing ways God has revealed Himself through prophecy, you'll gain a new appreciation for the incredible future He has planned for you.

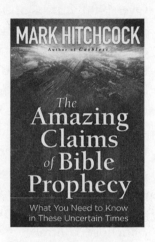

THE MAYAN APOCALYPSE
(a novel coauthored with Alton Gansky)

While searching for the answers to the meaning of life, Andrew Morgan encounters the ancient Mayan predictions that the world will end in 2012. When global disasters strike, Andrew cannot help but ask: Is everyone destined to a holocaust from which there is no escape?

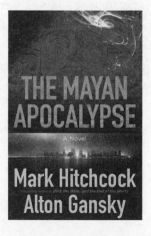